American Nightmares

American Nightmares

*Social Problems
in an Anxious World*

JOEL BEST

UNIVERSITY OF CALIFORNIA PRESS

University of California Press, one of the most distinguished university presses in the United States, enriches lives around the world by advancing scholarship in the humanities, social sciences, and natural sciences. Its activities are supported by the UC Press Foundation and by philanthropic contributions from individuals and institutions. For more information, visit www.ucpress.edu.

University of California Press
Oakland, California

Library of Congress Cataloging-in-Publication Data

Names: Best, Joel, author.
Title: American nightmares : social problems in an anxious world / Joel Best.
Description: Oakland, California : University of California Press, [2018] | Includes bibliographical references and index. |
Identifiers: LCCN 2017023300 (print) | LCCN 2017026171 (ebook) | ISBN 9780520968905 (Ebook) | ISBN 9780520296343 (cloth : alk. paper) | ISBN 9780520296350 (pbk. : alk. paper)
Subjects: LCSH: Anxiety—Social aspects—United States. | United States—Social conditions.
Classification: LCC HM1027.U6 (ebook) | LCC HM1027.U6 B47 2018 (print) | DDC 306.0973—dc23
LC record available at https://lccn.loc.gov/2017023300

Manufactured in the United States of America

25 24 23 22 21 20 19 18 17
10 9 8 7 6 5 4 3 2 1

For Eric

Contents

List of Illustrations ix

Acknowledgments xi

Preface xiii

PART ONE. CONTEMPORARY CONCERNS

1. Popular Hazards; or, How We Insist Similar Social
Problems Are Different

3

2. American Nightmares; or, Why Sociologists Hate the
American Dream
Written with David Schweingruber

34

PART TWO. CONSTRUCTING FUTURE PROBLEMS

3. Evaluating Predictions; or, How to Compare the Maya
Calendar, Social Security, and Climate Change

69

4. Future Talk; or, How Slippery Slopes Shape Concern

99

PART THREE. LOOKING BACKWARD
AND BEYOND SOCIOLOGY

5. Memories as Problems; or, How to Reconsider
Confederate Flags and Other Symbols of the Past
Written with Lawrence T. Nichols

129

6. Economicization; or, Why Economists Get More
Respect Than Sociologists

159

Afterword: The Future of American Nightmares 187

References 195

Index 225

Illustrations

FIGURES

1. *The Drunkards Progress* *14*

2. Pyramids of harms *16*

3. Ngram analysis of references to "American dream" in Google Books in American English, 1920–2010 *39*

4. Number of articles in the *American Sociological Review* and the *American Journal of Sociology* that mention *inequality* per article mentioning *equality*, by decade, 1900–2009 *65*

5. Number of articles in the *New York Times* mentioning economists per article mentioning sociologists, by decade, 1920–2015 *168*

TABLE

1. Estimates for the scale of some popular hazards, listed in rough order of popularity *10*

Acknowledgments

A variety of people made suggestions that helped me improve these chapters. I fear I am forgetting some, but I know I need to thank Tammy Anderson, Eric Best, Karen Cerulo, Steven Fazzari, Kenneth Haas, Sasha Levitt, Nicole Lloyd, Larry Nichols, Will Saletan, Dave Schweingruber, Joshua Stout, Thomas Vander Ven, and Carol Wickersham.

As always, it was a pleasure to work with the University of California Press. In particular, I want to acknowledge the help of Naomi Schneider, Dore Brown, Bonita Hurd, and Renée Donovan.

A shorter version of chapter 1 appeared in *Sociological Forum* 32 (2017): 461–79.

Preface

Sociologists sometimes have unusual, even exotic backgrounds. I do not. I am a first-year baby boomer. My father saw combat in the Second World War; he married my mother less than a month after the war ended, and I was born fifty-one weeks later. After my father attended college on the GI Bill, my parents received a VA loan to buy a house in a brand-new subdivision of identical, three-bedroom, one-bath homes in Roseville, Minnesota. Those houses filled with families just like ours—headed by guys who'd served in the war, gotten married, finished school, and were starting to have kids.

All those new homeowners caused Roseville, part of the first ring of suburbs around St. Paul, to boom. When we moved in, Lexington Elementary School was an old building with four classrooms—first and second graders in one room, up through seventh and eighth graders in another. There was no kindergarten for me to attend. But Lexington added a wing the next year, and I attended first grade in a brand-new classroom. In the years that followed, they kept adding wings on to the school, so that each year I was in elementary school, my class met in a brand-new room. For years, educators continued scrambling to build facilities to handle all the boomers. My freshman year at the University of Minnesota, they added a whole campus on the west bank of the Mississippi River.

My background, in short, is middle American. I grew up in a Midwestern suburb, in a white, two-child family. My father wore a white shirt and tie to his job as a middle manager for a large corporation; my mother was a homemaker who sometimes taught adult-education night classes. We attended a Presbyterian church. There was nothing exotic about our lives.

Over the years, I have heard other sociologists describe families whose situations were like ours as privileged. I understand the point they're making: we weren't victims of racial discrimination; there were other families with less money; and so on. But describing their lives as privileged would have struck my parents as ridiculous. Rather, they saw their situation as, if not precarious, at least quite challenging. The great bulk of their savings was in the equity in that tract home. My folks managed to buy a new car every few years, but it was a Plymouth, not a Dodge or a DeSoto, let alone a Chrysler. They were relieved that their two sons could attend a state university within commuting distance. (I remember coming home one day and telling my mother that my high school counselor had suggested—God knows why—I might consider applying to Princeton. My mother didn't say a word, and I never brought the matter up again.) I suppose we thought of ourselves as comfortable, even lucky—there was plenty of food, and none of us had severe health problems—but we certainly did not consider ourselves privileged.

In many ways, my parents lived the American Dream. They were the first in their families to graduate from college; in fact, three of my grandparents left school after completing the eighth grade. My father had grown up on a farm; my mother had lived in a variety of small towns and cities. But my parents went on to own a house in the suburbs. They lived virtuous lives—they were honest, hardworking, thrifty people. They encouraged their children to do well in school and to aspire to more education. To be sure, they were the beneficiaries of historical shifts—the impending war led to my father being drafted off the farm, and he never went back. Instead, the federal government rewarded his military service with support that allowed him to attend college and then buy a home; and during the 1950s and 1960s, the Cold War led to the government contracts that supported his factory. So it wasn't *all* their own doing, but the choices they made certainly made a difference.

I look back on my parents' lives from a different century, a new millennium. As a sociologist—and just as a person who tries to follow current events—I am struck by the range of commentators warning that the world my parents helped build is threatened, that the whole house of cards is in danger of collapse. We are told that the next generation will not be able to live the American Dream, that things are getting—or at least on the verge of getting—worse, maybe a lot worse. The institutions that most of us count on are said to be imperiled; we are told that our schools are failing to teach our kids, that medical care may soon be harder to obtain, that we won't be able to count on Social Security or our retirement plans, that our homes— still the largest chunk of most people's net worth—may lose much of their value, and so on.

These scenarios are what I call American Nightmares, because they are the opposite of the American Dream. Instead of believing that the future is bright, we worry that it will be dark. American Nightmares are fears that middle America's way of life is threatened.

This anxiety isn't entirely new. I learned to read in the 1950s, and I took to reading with tremendous enthusiasm. I read children's books and comics, of course, but I also delved into the newspapers and magazines that found their way into our home. The news was filled with warnings: the St. Paul paper serialized J. Edgar Hoover's *Masters of Deceit*—a best-selling book about the threat of Communist subversion; and there was intense concern about juvenile delinquency, gang violence, and organized crime. The schools were held to be a mess: I remember asking my mother why a magazine article said Johnny couldn't read—who was Johnny, and why was he having reading problems? Once the Soviet Union launched *Sputnik,* no one could doubt that American schools were failing (my school adopted new, innovative ways to teach math and science—billed as part of a national campaign to catch up with the Russians). Commentators tend to dismiss the 1950s as a placid decade when most Americans were smug and self-satisfied; but while my parents reassured me that we would be okay, I remember lots of folks warning that there were American Nightmares just ahead.

I've heard about American Nightmares—those warnings that middle America is endangered—throughout my life. As I studied American history I realized that these concerns date back at least to the colonial era; worries about witches, immigrants, Catholics, alcohol, capitalism, labor unions, Communists, criminals, dime novels, comic books, movies, drugs, cults—the list is almost endless—have been a continual refrain in our culture. Notice that there is another reason to think of these worries as nightmares: like our personal nightmares (the bad dreams we have while asleep), these collective American Nightmares make us very anxious while we are immersed in them; but they also seem exaggerated, over-wrought, and rather silly when we look back on them. However sincere and frightened the citizens of Salem may have been about the threat posed by witches—or Hoover about the danger of Communist subversion—we now view their fears as misplaced.

But American Nightmares cannot be relegated to the past; they remain a central theme in our culture. I finished this book in early 2017, shortly after Donald Trump became president. Trump's entire campaign had emphasized American Nightmare images: he declared his candidacy by announcing that the American Dream was dead, and that immigrants from Mexico were violent criminals; his campaign slogan implied that America was no longer great; as the campaign continued, he emphasized the threats posed by Muslim extremist terrorists and by trade deals and government regulations that were killing American prosperity; his speech accepting the Republican nomination began by warning that "attacks on our police, and the terrorism in our cities, threaten our very way of life"; and his inaugural address declared that policy failures had led to "American carnage." In turn, Trump's critics also adopted nightmarish imagery: a *Philadelphia Inquirer* editorial said "the early days of the Trump administration are suggestive of a tin-pot dictatorship," and a *Salon* piece called Trump "a fascist authoritarian in the American mold," while the Internet and social media were even less restrained. Certainly civility is in short supply, and some commentators claim that all this negativity is unprecedented, yet American history has featured plenty of vituperative exchanges between political opponents. Outrage and alarm are fairly standard elements in our politics.

But the turmoil surrounding President Trump is just one entrée on the contemporary menu of American Nightmares.

The apocalyptic warnings from both Trump's supporters and his opponents resemble lots of other claims about our precarious future. Think of all the warnings about environmental hazards, economic uncertainties, terrible inequities, medical menaces, failing institutions, technologies out of control, wayward asteroids, and on and on. Popular culture routinely portrays future hellscapes filled with collapsed civilizations, environmental devastation, and hordes of zombies. At a time when life expectancies are longer and living standards are higher than at any other moment in human history, our confidence in our institutions is declining. We continue to hear that the world we live in is endangered, that it is unraveling or is about to unravel—or at least is at risk of unraveling, and that it could all fall apart.

Yet these American Nightmares are not a topic that has attracted much attention from sociologists, who often seem intent on promoting a different set of concerns. To be sure, there are studies of moral panics, which try to understand why people get caught up in this or that bizarre fear. But mainstream sociologists view moral panics as a minor topic in our discipline. Rather, a disproportionate share of our discipline's work focuses on society's poorest members. Admittedly, sociologists sometimes study women, or children, or the elderly, or members of ethnic minorities; but when you look at that research, it quickly becomes obvious that often the analysts are especially interested in women who are poor, children who are poor, and so on. And when sociologists have directed their attention at middle America, they haven't been terribly sympathetic. Often, middle-class people's lives tend to be portrayed as empty, alienated, focused on such meaningless activities as shopping and watching television. If a nightmarish reckoning lies ahead, these sociologists seem to imply, those folks will have only themselves to blame.

Perhaps because I come from middle-American stock, perhaps because I grew up to replicate my parents' lives—I married, had two sons, and owned a house in the suburbs—I have found myself interested in American Nightmares. Over the years, I have studied warnings about a variety of threats—including poisoned Halloween candy, missing children, satanic ritual abuse, freeway violence, gang initiation rites, random violence, road rage, failing schools, sex bracelets, and such. This book continues that line of research. It examines a variety of warnings that things have been getting bad and are on the verge of getting a lot worse. Our focus is popular concerns—the ways the media and advocates encourage ordinary people to frame their worries, particularly about their uncertain futures. I hope that examining particular claims and their features can help place our fears about American Nightmares in context.

Three themes run through the chapters in this book. The first is how we talk about various threats that pose American Nightmares, and about social problems more generally. Here, I hope to expand upon my earlier analyses of social-problems rhetoric. While we tend to envision social problems as real, objective conditions, they can be recognized, understood, and made real only through discourse, through what people say about them. When people argue that something ought to be recognized as an important social problem, as a threat to the American Dream, they must explain the nature of that problem, its extent, and its patterns in order to convince others that this is a big problem that deserves to be taken seriously. Whatever understanding we have of social problems is produced and shaped through such rhetoric. And this is doubly true when people worry about the future. By definition, the future has not yet happened; its contours can become visible to us only through claims about what we ought to fear. How can we be persuaded to worry about some future problem?

The future is the second theme that runs through these chapters. Most sociological research—and especially research on social problems—concerns the present or, less often, the past. This makes sense: it seems possible to try and learn what is happening or to understand what has already happened; we can collect, interpret, and evaluate data. In contrast, talking about the future seems more speculative—like gazing into a crystal ball. And yet claims about social problems often warn, not so much that things are bad, as that they are going to get much worse. Both the American Dream and the American Nightmare are visions of futures, one bright, the other bleak. In a sense, any claim about the future can be countered with skepticism: how can anyone claim to know what is going to happen? Given this uncertainty, how should we decide which projected futures deserve our concern? Sociologists, who tend to focus on studying the present, have given less thought to all the talk about social problems that invokes the future.

This book's third theme is about the ways sociologists think about social problems. I have been studying sociology for more than half a century, and during that time I have witnessed our discipline's evolution. The relative importance that sociologists place on different topics has shifted: studies of small-group behavior and voluntary associations—once prominent, high-prestige research topics—have lost their glamour, while research on gender and on social movements has come to attract far more attention than it once did. These shifts have been valuable, in that important topics that previously were neglected have received increased scrutiny. But there are inevitably disadvantages as well: when our attention concentrates on one set of topics, it is easy to downplay or even forget about others. Humans are fickle; their ideas and concerns change, and sociologists are no different from other humans. I hope that the chapters in this book will allow us to think about how some topics currently pre-occupy sociologists and about what else might deserve their attention.

These three themes—rhetoric, the future, and sociological priorities—run through this book's chapters, although the three are not equally front and center in each chapter. Rather, the book is divided into three parts. The first part—chapters 1 and 2—concerns debates over contemporary social issues, although these debates inevitably involve claims about what will happen in the future. Chapters 3 and 4—the second part—focus specifi-cally on how we construct future social problems. Finally, the third part—chapters 5 and 6—extend the analysis in new direc-tions: into the past, and beyond the domain of sociology.

The first chapter explores the challenges of discussing popu-lar hazards—that is, things that are widely used, yet that carry risks (examples include cars, guns, and marijuana). There are many popular hazards. While these pose essentially the same policy challenge—how to address popular demand while mini-mizing risks—various popular hazards are viewed very differ-ently, both by the general public and by sociologists. Some are taken for granted (we accept the risks posed by automobiles), while others are much more controversial (consider debates about whether access to guns ought to be restricted, or whether recreational marijuana should be legalized). This chapter focuses on the rhetoric used to justify or denounce particular popular hazards. Often, these claims warn that the wrong policy choices could have devastating consequences for the future. And sociolo-gists can get caught up in this confusion, endorsing some popular hazards even as they reject others. This chapter asks whether recognizing the underlying similarities in the challenges posed by different popular hazards might not clarify policy debates, and whether less alarmist rhetoric might not be in order.

Chapter 2 concerns sociologists' distaste for the American Dream, which they tend to invoke as a straw figure that not merely ignores but actually can be blamed for inequities in our society. The American Dream is an important idea that many people use to understand both their own prospects and our nation's future. Yet many sociologists seem to view the American Dream as a dangerous fantasy that encourages complacency and even justifies inequality. I argue that this interpretation misunderstands the American Dream, which is, as its very name suggests, an aspiration or ideal. In fact, the term's ambiguity means that different people can define the American Dream in very different ways, which leads to lots of disagreement about what the American Dream is and how we ought to think about it. Moreover, all sorts of critics insist that the American Dream's future seems bleak, and this is certainly true for most sociologists, whose critiques of the American Dream often wind up exaggerating the rigidity of American social structure.

In the third and fourth chapters, the focus is squarely on the ways future problems are constructed. Chapter 3 invites us to think about the worried rhetoric used to construct future problems. It examines public reactions to three alarming predictions: that the Maya calendar foretold that the world would end in 2012; that Social Security is going to become insolvent in the near future; and that climate change poses a catastrophic threat to human civilization. Comparing these three claims will allow us to think about the sorts of evidence used to construct predictions of future social problems, and to consider ways in which policy debates about the future can be framed. Dealing with the future is anything but straightforward.

Chapter 4, too, deals with rhetoric about future problems, but it concentrates particularly on what we'll call future talk—on some everyday expressions we use to depict the future. Thus, it takes some common rhetorical ploys—warnings that X will lead to a slippery slope, that Y is just the tip of the iceberg, or that we are just beginning to see cases of Z—and asks how these expressions help give commonsense shape to the social problems of the future. These expressions draw on cultural resources; they help turn the amorphous future into something that seems to have familiar contours.

In chapter 5, we shift our focus from how we make sense of the future to how our collective memories of the past can become problematic. Recently, the meanings of the Confederate battle flag, as well as of memorials to the Confederacy and to the legacies of other historical figures, have come under attack, with some calling for expunging controversial memorials, while others defend them. Once again, the claims use distinctive rhetoric. These debates raise much bigger questions about shifts in the larger culture, and about the ways that the past can become a social problem in the present.

Finally, chapter 6 turns to what might seem to be a very different topic: how economists appear to be having more success than sociologists in shaping debates about social problems. But once again, we focus of the rhetoric adopted by these different social scientific disciplines. I argue that sociologists' current concerns have become narrow and predictable, whereas economists are having more success in drawing attention to their discipline's applicability to a wide range of topics, often with surprising results. By considering the limitations of sociological rhetoric, I hope to raise some concerns about our discipline's future.

Although they might appear to deal with very different, seemingly unrelated, topics, these six chapters convey my interest in the rhetoric—the social-problems talk—used to warn about a troubling future, about American Nightmares. They also speak to the challenges, and the possibilities, for sociologists who want to think about these claims. A brief afterword makes some of these connections explicit.

PART ONE

Contemporary Concerns

Popular Hazards; or, How We Insist Similar Social Problems Are Different

Consider things people do that might—but usually don't—result in harm. A partial list includes driving a car, owning or shooting a gun, drinking alcohol, smoking tobacco, having sexual intercourse, riding a motorcycle or a bicycle, using a credit card, owning a pit bull, gambling, eating junk food, consuming pornography, logging onto the Internet, and using illegal drugs. All of these are widespread activities. Some are legal, a few are or have been illegal, and several are regulated in various ways so that they are legal under some circumstances but not others. Lots of people do these things and cause little or no harm. Still, in some small proportion of cases, those engaged in these activities wind up harming—even killing—themselves or other people.

Think about cars. Automobiles are so ubiquitous that we measure traffic fatality rates per 100 million miles driven. In recent years, Americans have driven about 3 *trillion* miles annually. Although there are only about 1.1 fatalities per 100 million miles driven, that still works out to a fairly high body count—more than 32,000 deaths each year. Put that another way: every year, there is a traffic fatality for every 10,000 Americans (National Center for Statistics and Analysis 2014). We make a trade-off: in exchange for the tremendous freedom and convenience that cars permit, we tolerate these deaths.*

How should we think about this traffic death toll? Imagine someone announcing a wonderful new invention that would make enormous improvements in virtually every person's life but would kill more than 30,000 Americans each year. Would we be more likely to welcome this new invention or to ban it?

Of course, we have an array of social policies designed to minimize traffic fatalities. We license cars after inspecting them and certifying that they are in reasonably good condition, and license drivers after testing to make sure they understand and can follow basic traffic laws. We require cars to have safety features—not just seat belts and airbags but also electric turn signals, padded dashboards, and the like—and we require manufacturers to recall vehicles found to have dangerous equipment. We design roads to safely handle traffic at posted speed limits. We have raised the minimum ages at which drivers can be licensed, introduced graduated licenses imposing special restrictions on the youngest drivers, cracked down on drivers arrested for driving under the influence of alcohol, and made it tougher for aging drivers to renew their licenses. And these policies work. In 1966, there were 50,894 traffic fatalities. In the intervening half century, the U.S. popula-

---

* This trade-off can be seen in policy changes: Friedman, Hedeker, and Richter (2009) estimate that raising speed limits above fifty-five miles per hour increased fatalities by 3.23 percent—an additional 12,545 deaths over the first ten years that higher limits were in effect—without inspiring widespread calls for a return to lower limits.

tion grew, as did the number of drivers and the number of miles they drove, yet the national traffic death toll actually declined and the fatality rate dropped 80 percent, from 5.5 per 100 million miles driven in 1966 to 1.1 in 2010 (National Highway Traffic Safety Administration 2013).

Yet people continue to die on the roadways. Much of this reflects unwise, often illegal behavior: drivers speed and drive recklessly; they don't buckle up; they drink and drive; or they text or allow themselves to be distracted in other ways. Those with good driving habits are undoubtedly at much lower risk than those who are more adventurous or foolhardy. Perhaps this is one reason we accept the highway death toll. While we know that tragedy can strike anyone who happens to be on the road in the wrong place at the wrong time, we also know that a car is usually a reasonably safe way to travel.*

Notice, too, that people continue to debate traffic policies. There are advocates who call for even safer cars or tougher laws, as well as those who worry about automobiles' environmental harms and call for shifting to bicycles, mass transit, or greener cars. Others argue that current policies are too restrictive: teenagers resent today's later legal driving ages and graduated licenses that did not apply to earlier generations; manufacturers

---

* Risks and policies for managing them have varied histories. Thus, Mohun (2013) traces the emergence of policies governing automobiles, guns, and amusement parks, among other risks. Vardi (2014) argues that the harms caused by early automobiles inspired moral outrage, but that those deaths came to be normalized by cars' advocates who emphasized the relative infrequency of fatalities compared to the volume of traffic, thereby redefining these harms as a technical problem to be addressed through engineering improvements. The different histories of different risks help us understand how cultural and structural contingencies at different historical moments can help explain the range of ways popular hazards have been defined and addressed and how different social policies have been devised.

object to the costs of building cars that meet new safety standards; and some drivers call for higher speed limits. Because we live in, not just a car culture that celebrates automobility, but also a geographically big country in which most people's daily lives depend on having ready access to cars, these debates aren't all that loud. While the future may feature cars that drive themselves or don't burn petroleum, it is difficult to imagine that we will stop relying on cars of some sort anytime soon.

POPULAR HAZARDS

Cars are a *popular hazard*—popular in the sense that many millions of people own and use them, yet a hazard in that they also involve real dangers and harm some people. In calling them *popular,* I intend to convey two qualities: first, I am referring to common activities involving lots of people; and second, these activities often engage those people on some emotional level—they are things that people enjoy or value, and that they would prefer to continue doing. Cars, for instance, are popular in both senses: many millions of people drive cars; and, beyond valuing cars' utilitarian qualities, many of those people are attached to driving—they depend on being able to do it, but they also enjoy it and may even build their identities around cars (think of lowriders, hot-rodders, sports car enthusiasts, and NASCAR fans). By referring to popular *hazards,* I acknowledge that these activities involve real risks, that they do lead to harm for some people, including those killed or injured in traffic accidents.

The category of popular hazards includes many of the deviant exchanges Schur (1965) called *crimes without victims,* such as illegal drug deals and illicit sexual exchanges, but it is much broader.* Many popular hazards are perfectly legal. Think about drinking alcohol or using credit cards: most people manage to do these things legally and without serious problems, but small proportions of drinkers and credit-card users wind up ruining their lives. Guns are not that different: there are probably more than 300 million working firearms in the United States (nearly half of Americans live in households with guns), yet only a tiny fraction of those guns wind up hurting people.

Describing popular hazards in this way might seem to emphasize their objective qualities, but of course these phenomena are understood—constructed—through subjective processes (Best 2017; Loseke 2003; Spector and Kitsuse 1977). All cognitive categories are produced through social interaction, including our definitions of what is a car—or a harm. Analysts necessarily bracket some categories and accept the relevance of social context. In order to proceed to more interesting issues, we

---

* While Schur's analysis was influential, the very term *crimes without victims* invited critics to dispute the claim that no one was victimized by these crimes. Schur's point—that deviant exchanges were organized differently from deviant exploitation—became lost as critics pounded the table and declared, "X is not a victimless crime! It has victims!" (cf. Martin 2015; Farley and Malarek 2008).

The concept of popular hazards is a way of circumventing two problems with Schur's term. The first, of course, is that talking about *victims*—and particularly *victimless crimes*—proved to be a red herring, leading people to focus on debating who qualifies as a victim and the nature of various forms of victimization, and to search for evidence that deviant exchanges did indeed victimize some people. In contrast, speaking of hazards acknowledges that people run the risk of being harmed, and that if enough people take some risk, it is a near certainty that we will be able to point to people who have been harmed. The second problem with Schur's term is that it speaks of crimes. This was appropriate for his analysis, in that he was criticizing what he saw as overreaching criminalization, but not all popular hazards are criminalized.

can agree that there are a great many cars, and that using them is understood to involve substantial harms. That is, we can accept that popular hazards are activities recognized as being both popular and hazardous, and move on to consider how, within that cultural context, people construct claims for dealing with such activities.

Analyses of social-problems construction tend to be case studies that focus on particular claimsmaking campaigns (Best 2015). Comparisons tend to be modest; they examine claims about the same troubling condition made at different times or in different places, or about different conditions that share some underlying theme (e.g., threats to children), or that are made by claimsmakers who share an ideology (e.g., feminism). But the concept of popular hazards invites us to compare the construction of cases that might seem to have very little in common. On the surface, popular hazards seem to be very different from one another: they span a continuum from legal to forbidden; some are the focus of active policy debates, while others seem to attract little attention, let alone concern; and different popular hazards are viewed as problematic—or not—by very different sectors of society. It is not uncommon for individuals to support restrictions on some popular hazards, even as they oppose restricting others.

The category of popular hazards draws our attention to the social context—the social organization of activities—within which social problems are constructed. Popularity and hazardousness can be understood in different ways. Is an activity's popularity a sign that it is a legitimate part of our culture, or evidence that there is a major problem? Are harms a regrettable but inevitable cost of having a popular choice, or unnecessary and intolerable? The question is: How can we explain the very different ways we understand and deal with various popular hazards?

Discussions of popular hazards usually proceed on a case-by-case basis: we talk about regulating cars and about regulating guns, and we view each of those conversations as unrelated to the other. I want to consider whether we can understand these debates better if we think about them as instances of the broader category of popular hazards, and whether we can find patterns in the rhetoric adopted in advocates' campaigns about apparently unrelated issues. We can begin by identifying some important similarities among these apparently disparate phenomena, then explore patterns in the rhetoric people use to understand popularity and hazardousness.

MEASURING THE MAGNITUDES OF POPULARITY AND HAZARDOUSNESS

Just how popular—and how hazardous—are popular hazards? Table 1 gives some rough estimates, located through online searches. These statistics come from a variety of sources, and they need to be handled with care. Some data are counts, collected or compiled systematically by government agencies, and should be fairly accurate, but even here caution is in order. For instance, we can probably have reasonable confidence in the number of licensed drivers because we know that states make an effort to ensure that all drivers are licensed and keep records of the number of active licenses (if only to collect the licensing fees), and there are penalties for driving without a license. Still, even this pretty-good figure has problems. Some states have had debates about whether undocumented immigrants should be eligible to receive licenses (Stewart 2012). Prohibiting individuals from receiving driver's licenses is no guarantee that they will not drive, and enough unlicensed drivers escape notice to

TABLE I

Estimates for the Scale of Some Popular Hazards, Listed in Rough Order of Popularity

	Estimates of Popularity	Estimates of Serious Harms
Automobiles	Licensed drivers: 210,000,000 (2010)[a]	Traffic fatalities (includes motorcyclists): 32,719 (2013)[b]
Gambling	Americans who gamble: >80% (~192,000,000 adults) (2012)[c]	Pathological gamblers: 2,500,000 (1999)[d]
Credit cards	Americans with a credit card: 72.1% (~173,000,000 adults) (2012)[e]	Adults rolling over more than $10,000 in credit card debt: 6% (~15 million adults) (2014)[f]
Alcohol	Those 18+ who had a drink in the previous year: 70% (~172,000,000 adults) (2014)[g]	Deaths from alcohol-related causes: 88,000 (2013)[g] Adults with an alcohol use disorder: 16,600,000 (2013)[g]
Marijuana	Adults reporting having used marijuana: 49% (~122,000,000) (2015)[h]	Primary substance abuse treatment admissions for marijuana: 321,648 (2008)[i]
Firearms	Americans who own a gun: 34% (~81,000,000 adults) (2011)[j] Households with a gun: 47% (2011)[j]	Deaths from firearms: 33,636 (2013)[k]
Pornography	18–39-year-olds viewing pornography during previous year: males—69%; females—40% (~49,000,000 plus older adults) (2015)[l]	Pornography addicts: 200,000 (2012)[m]
Cigarettes	Cigarette smokers: 40,000,000 (2014)[n]	Deaths from cigarette smoking: 480,000 (includes 40,000 caused by secondhand smoke) (2014)[n]
Bicycles	Number riding bicycle at least six times in previous year: 40,000,000 (2010)[o]	Number of fatalities in bicycle-related traffic accidents: 743[p]

Motorcycles	Registered motorcycles: 7,138,476 (2007)[q]	Motorcyclist fatalities: 4,668 (2013)[b]
Pit bulls	Registered pit bulls: 5,000,000 (2014)[r]	Fatal pit bull attacks: 22 (2011)[s]

[a] Office of Highway Policy Information (2012).
[b] National Highway Traffic Safety Administration (2013).
[c] Research Institute on Addictions (2012).
[d] National Opinion Research Center (1999).
[e] Schuh and Stavins (2014).
[f] Swift (2014).
[g] National Institute on Alcohol Abuse and Alcoholism (2015).
[h] Motel (2015).
[i] Center for Behavioral Health Statistics and Quality (2010).
[j] Saad (2011).
[k] Centers for Disease Control and Prevention (2015a).
[l] Regnerus, Gordon, and Price (2016).
[m] Webroot.com (2015).
[n] Centers for Disease Control and Prevention (2015b).
[o] Edmondson (2011).
[p] Centers for Disease Control and Prevention (2015c).
[q] Morris (2009).
[r] Flanagin (2014).
[s] DogsBite.org (2015).

account for about one-eighth of drivers involved in fatal crashes (Foundation for Traffic Safety 2011).

Other statistics are clearly rough estimates. Because firearms need not be registered, it is impossible to know the number of guns in working order. Nor do gun owners need to be licensed, so statistics on gun ownership come from surveys asking whether the respondent—or someone in the respondent's household— owns a gun. But we can imagine that some people may not answer such questions honestly, either refusing to acknowledge that they own a gun or claiming to own guns when they do not.

Some of these figures are contentious, and estimates may come from advocates likely to favor numbers that seem to support their positions (Best 2012). In general, those who endorse some popular hazard are likely to favor high estimates of its popularity and low estimates of its harms, while critics of the same hazard may prefer estimates that minimize its popularity and maximize its harms. In short, none of the numbers in table 1 can be considered perfectly accurate, yet we can still use them to get a general sense of the extent of the popularity and hazardousness of various popular hazards.

This is because the overall pattern in table 1 is quite clear. The left-hand column shows that, for each of the popular hazards listed in the table, the estimates of popularity are in the millions; for the most part, tens—if not hundreds—of millions of people are involved with each of these popular hazards. The number of people exposed to the hazards' risks must be even larger: roughly two-thirds of Americans are licensed drivers, but the vast majority of those who do not themselves drive find themselves passengers riding in motor vehicles or pedestrians walking on or near roads. Some estimates of harm specifically include those who are not directly involved in the hazard; for instance, table 1's estimate for tobacco-related deaths includes victims of secondhand smoke.

Neither a popular hazard's popularity nor its associated risks need be distributed evenly across society. People make decisions to smoke tobacco or drink alcohol, or to own a gun—or to not do those things—and there are large social scientific literatures showing how age, gender, race and ethnicity, social class, religiosity, and other variables affect rates of involvement in different popular hazards (cf. Slovic 2000, 2010). Risks and harms also are unevenly distributed. For many popular hazards, a disproportionate share of harms are experienced by young males (sometimes identified as being most "at risk"), and there are other large literatures offering explanations for the varying propensities to take—or at least be exposed to—risks. For instance, inexperience with a popular hazard may make it harder to assess and manage its dangers. This helps explain the many programs designed to give the young formal instruction in risks and the need for thoughtful decision-making, such as sex education, driver education, and alcohol and drug education.

The right-hand column of table 1 reveals two things: first, in most cases substantial numbers—tens or even hundreds of thousands, and in some cases millions—of people can be considered harmed by each of the popular hazards; but, second, the numbers harmed are relatively small fractions of those involved.* Thus, compared to the ubiquity of automobiles, relatively few people die in traffic accidents. Debates over popular hazards revolve around this basic issue: What should be done about things that are extremely popular but which also cause substantial damage? How should we weigh their costs and benefits? That is, we must consider the rhetoric people use in policy debates about popular hazards.

ARRAYS OF HARMS

Critics of popular hazards often invoke melodramatic warnings. Figure 1 presents a classic 1846 print from Currier and Ives titled *The Drunkard[']s Progress*.† It depicts a deviant career, an arc of nine

---

* There are various ways to conceptualize harm, some of which may make a popular hazard seem more or less harmful. For example, over a lifetime of exposure to some popular hazard, the cumulative risk of harm can seem substantial. It is estimated that smoking contributes to the early deaths of between one-third (Mattson, Pollack, and Cullen 1987) and two-thirds (Banks et al. 2015) of smokers. On the other hand, Gusfield (1993: 67) suggests that presenting absolute risks (the increased chance that a smoker will die within a particular time period) produces smaller numbers that make the risk seem less impressive.

† Such depictions of destructive deviant careers were not new: a century earlier William Hogarth published the series of engravings *The Harlot's*

Figure 1. *The Drunkards Progress* (Currier and Ives, 1846). Source: Library of Congress.

stages through which a drunkard proceeds, beginning with "A glass with a Friend" and ending with "Death by suicide"; in the background we see an abandoned wife and small child, their home in ruins. This plot of self-destruction is familiar: when advocates warn about the seductive, corrupting experiences that endanger youths who experiment with alcohol, tobacco, sex, gambling, or marijuana ("the gateway drug"), they are warning that first missteps may—perhaps quite often—lead to terrible consequences.

Obviously, Currier and Ives's drunkard represents a worst-case scenario. Many, many people share a drink with a friend, but

---

Progress and *The Rake's Progress,* which tracked the self-destructive paths of a young woman and a young man, respectively.

relatively few go on to kill themselves. Suicide is not a certain, or even a particularly likely, outcome of drinking. A drinking career should not be conceptualized as a sort of railroad track that leads inevitably to the next, ever-more-terrible station. There are options—every opportunity to drink offers a choice, and people's choices lead to a broad array of outcomes. Some people never drink alcohol, others drink on rare occasions or in limited amounts; some may drink enough to become impaired, but only infrequently. And we also speak of functioning alcoholics who drink regularly and may depend on alcohol yet manage to avoid wrecking their lives, as well as of recovering alcoholics who halt their drinking and focus on not resuming. Every popular hazard involves a similar range of outcomes.

The drunkard's suicide is certainly a devastating consequence, as are fatal outcomes of other popular hazards, such as gunshots and traffic accidents. But most popular hazards involve a range of harms. As a general rule, the more devastating the harm, the rarer it is. For any popular hazard, we can envision a pyramid of harms, with a broad base denoting the most common but least serious harms, with successive layers, each narrower and representing increasingly serious but decreasingly common harms, until we reach a fairly narrow peak representing the relatively small number of devastating harms. Figure 2 illustrates this pattern using motor vehicle accidents and firearm incidents as examples.

Again, all of the numbers in figure 2 are likely to be flawed, although the number of deaths in each case—the most serious category of harms in both cases—is likely to be fairly accurate, because dead bodies tend to be noticed and counted. On the other hand, we can suspect that even large numbers of the least serious incidents—traffic accidents without injuries and crimes

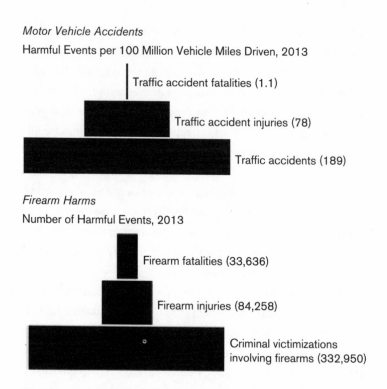

Motor Vehicle Accidents
Harmful Events per 100 Million Vehicle Miles Driven, 2013

Traffic accident fatalities (1.1)

Traffic accident injuries (78)

Traffic accidents (189)

Firearm Harms
Number of Harmful Events, 2013

Firearm fatalities (33,636)

Firearm injuries (84,258)

Criminal victimizations
involving firearms (332,950)

Figure 2. Pyramids of harms: more serious harms are less common. Sources: *Motor vehicle accidents*—National Center for Statistics and Analysis (2014); *firearm fatalities and injuries*—Centers for Disease Control and Prevention (2014); *criminal victimizations involving firearms*—Truman and Langton (2014).

involving firearms, respectively—might never come to the attention of the officials trying to tally these incidents. In other words, both pyramids may well be considerably broader at their bases than figure 2 suggests.

It is also worth remarking that, although the two graphs in the figure use different measurement scales, the absolute numbers of deaths attributed to traffic accidents in 2013 (32,719) is very close to that year's number of firearm deaths (33,636). However, when comparing the least serious harms, there are vastly more instances involving motor vehicle accidents without injuries (5.6 million) than firearms-related crimes without injuries (332,950). In other words, while it seems likely that all popular hazards will feature this pyramid of harms, the ratio of the most serious to the least serious harms may vary a great deal. Even when the number of devastating harms seems impressive, it will be dwarfed by cases involving less serious harms.

In some cases, it may be hard to agree on just what constitutes harm. For instance, many people who have credit cards pay their full balance each month, so they never pay interest on their credit card purchases. We can argue that credit cards offer them convenience without harm (so long as we ignore the higher prices merchants must charge to cover the fees that the credit card companies exact from each purchase and the ways cards promote a culture of consumption). But other people carry over a portion of their balance each month, and they can wind up paying substantial interest charges. At what point should we declare this to be harmful? Table 1 estimates that about 6 percent of adults with credit cards carry over balances that exceed ten thousand dollars. Some of those folks will wind up declaring bankruptcy (and no doubt a few may, like our drunkard, take their own lives in the face of overwhelming debts), but many others will manage to pay off their balances without lasting consequences.

Understanding these patterns is important, because people who call attention to a social problem are likely to typify that problem by pointing to fatalities and other instances of devastating harm (Best 1990, 2017). But this does not necessarily help us devise social policies or even think clearly about these issues. Even if it is the case that some drinkers who begin their drinking career by sharing a glass with friends do in fact go on to kill themselves, it is not clear what we ought to do about this: Develop alcohol education programs to warn people about the risks of drinking? Offer counseling and other services to individuals who have trouble managing their drinking? Or perhaps ban alcohol altogether? Acknowledging the drunkard's suicide does not help us choose among the array of policy options.

RHETORIC ABOUT POPULAR HAZARDS

The harms and the benefits of popular hazards become the subject of social-problems claims. While these tend to take the form of problem-specific claims (e.g., Because popular hazard X has beneficial/harmful consequence Y, we should adopt policy Z), we can recognize that many popular hazards inspire analogous claims with similar rhetoric among both those who defend some popular hazard (who tend to emphasize its popularity and downplay its hazardousness) and those who call for policies to restrict or ban the hazard (who tend to highlight its harms even as they discount its popularity).

In order to illustrate the sorts of rhetoric common in these debates, I use claims from two contemporary debates about social issues: whether recreational marijuana use should be legalized; and whether tighter gun control policies should be implemented. My examples present rhetoric from popular sources—websites, articles in the press, and trade books aimed at general audiences. Both issues have also inspired scholarly literatures that feature debates between proponents and opponents, but these claims tend to be obscured by academic language. Claims in the public square are more overt, so it is easier to recognize the rhetorical moves being made.

I chose the examples of gun control and legal marijuana precisely because many people are inclined to favor allowing access to one of these popular hazards but not the other: that is, many political liberals are likely to favor relaxing restrictions on marijuana while tightening restrictions on guns; and many political conservatives are more likely to favor maintaining the restrictions on marijuana while opposing tighter restrictions on guns.* This suggests that people may find the same line of reasoning—a rhetorical device—convincing when it is presented in one debate yet unpersuasive in the other. Such inconsistent reactions reveal that social-problems claims rely on something more than straightforward argumentative logic or coherent philosophical principles.

Claims Defending Popular Hazards

Those who advocate decriminalization of, or defend, some popular hazard tend to invoke a fairly standard set of arguments:

A. that it is indeed popular: that it is used/enjoyed by large numbers of people;

B. that most of those people are respectable and use it responsibly;

C. that they may depend on being able to use it;

D. that it involves minimal risks, so long as it is used responsibly;

E. that it is possible to discourage its irresponsible use;

F. that people should have the right to use/enjoy it;

G. that it has long had a place in the larger culture;

* Compare Pew Research Center (2013, 2014) data showing that more Democrats than Republicans favor both legalizing marijuana (59 to 37 percent) and controlling gun ownership (65 to 24 percent).

H. that it is similar to other popular hazards that are
   socially accepted; and

I. that trying to ban it is likely to do more harm than good.

Consider our two examples. For decades, advocates for legalizing marijuana have pointed to evidence showing that many
millions of Americans have smoked marijuana (A); that most of
them are otherwise law-abiding citizens (B); that this widespread use has continued for many decades (G); that some people depend on marijuana for its medicinal benefits (C); that marijuana's effects resemble and are no more harmful than those of
alcohol (D, H); that people should have the right to choose
whether they use it (F); that efforts to ban marijuana have had
many deleterious consequences (e.g., turning many smokers into
criminals who feel contemptuous of the law, increasing prison
populations, and fostering organized criminality to supply the
drug [I]); and that a wiser policy would be to legalize the drug
while penalizing irresponsible use (e.g., to prohibit driving while
high [E]; cf. Kaplan 1970; Fox, Armentano, and Tvert 2009).

Similarly, the National Rifle Association and other pro-gun
advocates make a parallel set of claims: that there are millions of
law-abiding gun owners (A, B); that many of them depend on
guns to protect themselves (C); that guns are safe when used
responsibly (D); that laws can discourage irresponsible use (e.g.,
by having stricter penalties for those who commit crimes involving the use of a firearm [E]); that the Second Amendment guar-
antees the right to bear arms (F); that owning guns is an American tradition (G); that guns are not that different from other
popular hazards (H); and that banning guns would have harmful
consequences (e.g., depriving law-abiding citizens of the ability
to protect themselves [I]; cf. LaPierre 1994; Poe 2001).

Thus, there are clear rhetorical parallels between those working to make marijuana use more acceptable (a cause that tends to enlist politically liberal supporters), and those opposing greater restrictions on gun ownership (usually viewed as a politically conservative position). This means many individuals find one of these sets of claims persuasive, even as they reject the other set as unfounded—so consistent principles of political ideology rarely guide thinking about popular hazards. (Libertarianism seems to be an exception, in that libertarians generally favor policies that permit access to popular hazards.) Nor is there anything atypical about the arguments used to defend marijuana and guns; it is easy to identify analogous claims among those defending gambling, tobacco, alcohol, and so on. Those who defend some popular hazard tend to acknowledge the risks but argue that they are manageable and that the popular hazard's benefits outweigh its costs.

In general, inertia (Becker 1995) favors those who would defend widely popular hazards that are well integrated into existing social arrangements. Popular hazards such as these are unlikely to be banned outright, although they may be subjected to additional restrictions designed to minimize their harms.* For example, the ubiquity of cars, the centrality of automobility in contemporary culture and social structure, and the huge costs and other practical obstacles to eliminating motor vehicles make it difficult to envision campaigns against cars succeeding. At the same time, there have been many successful efforts to regulate driving in order to reduce the harms cars cause. Or, to take a second example, tobacco smok-

---

* The obvious exception is Prohibition (cf. McGirr 2016). However, the campaign to make drink illegal took decades and involved establishing an unstable political coalition with disparate elements. The policy cut—but fell far short of eliminating—alcohol consumption and was abandoned as unworkable about a dozen years later.

ing has not been banned, but it has been discouraged through countless federal, state, and local policy changes, such as higher tobacco taxes, restrictions on where cigarettes can be purchased and smoked, and limits on tobacco advertising. The percentage of people who smoke has been cut roughly in half, just as highway traffic-death tolls have fallen dramatically. These successful campaigns have set modest goals: they have sought to reduce the harms from these very popular hazards rather than to ban them.

In contrast, those defending popular hazards that are officially forbidden find that inertia works against them. For instance, advocates calling for legalizing marijuana have been making the same, heavily publicized arguments for half a century—efforts that only now seem to be gaining some traction. Most states have adopted medical marijuana programs, and a handful have decriminalized recreational marijuana possession, sale, and use (although it seems unlikely that federal law is about to change in the near future). This suggests that efforts to end bans against popular hazards also face the constraints of inertia.

Claims Opposing Popular Hazards

In general, those who advocate tougher restrictions on popular hazards are particularly likely to emphasize the harms they cause. They point to evidence of people killed, injured, or otherwise harmed. This is not difficult. Popular hazards are popular, often engaging many millions of people, and if only a small fraction of those millions suffer harms, this may still add up to tens or hundreds of thousands—even millions—of people being harmed. The issue is how to present these harms in a compelling manner.

The simplest method for constructing a popular hazard's harmfulness is to offer typifying examples of people harmed by the popular hazard (Best 1990, 2017). For example, the website for Citizens Against Legalizing Marijuana (CALM 2015a) declares, "Sure, marijuana may have never killed anyone as proponents often claim—just as a bottle of whiskey has never killed anyone,"* and then offers links to several news reports illustrating instances of marijuana use leading to serious harms:

> Here's some examples of people killing and maiming others when under the influence of marijuana with or without combining with alcohol:
>
> 16 year old Teen Dies after Rolling Car off Cliff—Marijuana in System ...
>
> Woman Kills Self and 7 others While High on Marijuana ...
>
> Man Attacks Flight Crew after Eating Marijuana Cookies ...
>
> "Psychotic Pothead" Shoots Pentagon Police ...

Similarly, advocates for gun control routinely point to heavily publicized mass shootings, such as Columbine and Sandy Hook. Of course, both sets of typifying examples are chosen primarily because they offer compelling stories; they almost always feature extreme, atypical incidents.

A second method is simply to emphasize the large number of people harmed by the popular hazard.† Thus, gun-control advocates point to the more than 30,000 annual firearm fatalities (a total that includes homicides, suicides, and accidental shootings). They present this as a big number, indicative of a big prob-

---

* Note the parallel claim by gun control's opponents: "Guns don't kill people. People kill people." In general, opponents of some popular hazard are more likely to speak of it as though it directly causes harm, while proponents are more likely to challenge such language.

† On the importance of big numbers, see Best (2012). It is also possible to make much of less common harms. Fatalities caused by dog bites are rare. However, claims about the dangers posed by pit bulls emphasize that the

lem, even offering comparative statistics to suggest that this is a much larger number than fatalities from some other serious problem. Thus, in the aftermath of a shooting at an Oregon college, President Obama (2015) made this request: "I would ask news organizations ... [to] tally up the number of Americans who have been killed in terrorist attacks over the last decade and the number of Americans who've been killed by gun violence, and post those side by side on your news reports." CNN, for instance, responded by calculating that there had been 406,496 "deaths by firearms on U.S. soil" versus 3,380 "deaths by terrorism" (United States and overseas attacks targeting Americans) between 2001 and 2013 (Jones and Bower 2015; see also Qui 2015). The choice of comparison makes all the difference; those seeking to highlight guns' hazardousness are of course much less likely to contrast firearm fatalities to deaths caused by automobility (more than 500,000 over the same period).

Opponents of marijuana legalization also use statistics to evoke the magnitude of the problem legalized marijuana poses. Thus, CALM claims, "In 2006, there were 290,563 marijuana-related emergency room visits, more than for all [other] drugs combined," and "26.9% of seriously injured drivers test positive for marijuana and 20% of all vehicle crashes are attributed to drugged driving" (CALM 2015c,d). But such claims also ignore comparable statistics about the obvious comparison drug—alcohol (e.g., drinking accounts for more emergency-room visits for those under twenty-one than marijuana and all other drugs combined [Mothers Against Drunk Driving 2013]). Thus, we can see a straightforward

---

breed accounts for a disproportionate share of these deaths: "31 U.S. dog bite-related fatalities occurred in 2011.... [P]it bulls contributed to 71 percent (22) of these deaths. Pit bulls make up about 5 percent of the total U.S. dog population" (DogsBite.org 2015).

rhetorical strategy: pointing to comparisons where the popular hazard in question appears larger, while neglecting to mention comparisons that make the harms seem relatively less harmful.

Advocates seeking to establish statistical evidence of harm may also choose to focus on the victimization of sympathetic figures.* Children, because they are considered innocent, vulnerable, and therefore in need of adult protection, are particularly useful in this regard, and gun control advocates emphasize, not just school shootings, but also the number of children harmed by firearms. Thus, one blogger posted: "I've found at least 43 instances this year of somebody being shot by a toddler 3 or younger. In 31 of those 43 cases, a toddler found a gun and shot himself or herself" (Ingraham 2015; see also Brady Center to Prevent Gun Violence 2016). According to the blogger's data, these incidents resulted in 15 deaths (as well as 28 injuries); since he published his statistics in mid-October, with roughly a quarter of the year remaining, we can estimate the annual toddler death toll from guns fired by themselves or another toddler at about 20. Each of these deaths is, of course, a tragedy, a product of terrible adult carelessness in leaving a gun where a small child could reach it. However, this claim seems strongest when presented in isolation. Small children suffer all sorts of fatal accidents. For example, in 2013, 214 children

---

* On the rhetorical importance of children, see Best (1990). Special restrictions seeking to protect young people from popular hazards are common. In the early 1970s—the same time that the voting age was reduced to eighteen—many states lowered their minimum drinking age. In the face of mounting evidence that there had been a dramatic increase in traffic fatalities among eighteen-to-twenty-year-olds, Mothers Against Drunk Driving and other advocates successfully campaigned to raise the national drinking age to twenty-one (although many states' laws allow younger people to drink under some circumstances). Research suggests that one effect of this policy change has been to reduce traffic fatalities by about nine hundred per year (DeJong and Blanchette 2014).

aged three or younger died in traffic accidents; at least 53 of those were not properly restrained in car seats and also might be constructed as victims of adult carelessness (National Center for Statistics and Analysis 2015); or, to take another example, during the period 2005 to 2009, more than 500 children aged four or under—about 100 per year—drowned in swimming pools (Centers for Disease Control and Prevention 2012). All of these deaths can be viewed as tragic failures of adult supervision. The point is not that guns kill fewer toddlers than cars or swimming pools, but that claims about popular hazards' dangers tend to zero in on particular risks to highlight those harms in isolation. In a society with lots of guns—and cars and swimming pools—there will inevitably be some harms, even to small children.

Similarly, opponents of legalizing recreational marijuana use also emphasize harms to the young. After all, marijuana smoking commonly begins during adolescence. For example, CALM warns: "Marijuana adversely affects memory, maturation, motivation and can cause irreversible impact on young brains that aren't fully developed until roughly age 25. It is a contributing factor in California's alarming high school drop-out rate.... More young people ages 12–17 entered drug treatment in 2003 for marijuana dependency than for alcohol and all other illegal drugs combined" (CALM 2015b). Another critic argues, "Both subtle and acute changes in emotional and intellectual development occur in young marijuana users because the arc of their brain's structural development becomes recalibrated by marijuana use" (Sabet 2013: 40), and cites a study which reports that "using marijuana regularly before age eighteen resulted in an average IQ of six to eight fewer points at age thirty-five" (42; see also Bennett and White 2015). In short, legalizing a drug that is commonly used by the young would imperil both the individual users and the larger society's human capital. Of course, these reported harms have occurred during a period when marijuana was illegal, and any laws legalizing recreational marijuana are likely to incorporate some sort of age limit on consumption. Therefore, it is hard to assess the degree to which legalization is likely to increase harms to the young. But, again, advocates rarely acknowledge—let alone confront—such critiques.

Other arguments may talk about broader—albeit less easily measured—harms. They may even acknowledge that the popular hazard in question has many users, and that relatively few of them wind up being harmed, while insisting that the harms are nonetheless severe enough to justify their opposition. For instance, one marijuana opponent argues, "It is true that most people who will one day smoke a joint will not become addicted or have major problems with marijuana—indeed many stop after using it once or twice. But the fact that a minority of users will experience significant negative health ramifications, including a significant loss in IQ and poor learning outcomes, lung damage, mental illness, motor skills impairment, and even addiction, offers plenty to worry about" (Sabet 2013: 26).

Similarly, the Brady Center to Prevent Gun Violence (2016) warns, "Keeping a gun in the home increases the risk of injury and death. Gun owners may overestimate the benefits of keeping a gun in the home and underestimate the risks." Such claims may briefly acknowledge popularity—that most people who smoke a joint will not become addicted, or that many gun owners believe that there are benefits to keeping a gun in the home—but opponents place the emphasis on demonstrating hazardousness.

Like the proponents of popular hazards, opponents must deal with inertia. Gun control advocates find themselves confronting a well-entrenched, politically influential gun lobby committed to blocking any further regulations, while marijuana's opponents must try to slow a pro-legalization movement that seems to have momentum, by warning against a "rush to legalize marijuana" (Bennett and White 2015).

Debates about Social Policies

The rhetorical similarities across issues extend to debates about social policies, even those that, at first glance, might seem to revolve around very different issues. Currently, opponents of legalizing the recreational use of marijuana warn of substantial social costs, while proponents insist that there will be minimal harms. This has led opponents to monitor the states that first legalized recreational use, watching for reports of harms. Thus, former federal drug czar William J. Bennett reports, regarding Colorado, that injury-causing explosions in laboratories for extracting THC have increased; that "two Denver deaths" have occurred, "one of a nineteen-year-old who jumped to his death while high, the other of a woman whose husband shot her after eating 'Karma Kandy'"; that children have wound up in emergency rooms after consuming edible marijuana; and that the state has seen "a sizable increase in marijuana-related DUI admissions to treatment centers." Lest this list of harms seem insufficient, he concludes: "The truth is that Colorado is *about to* wreak a great deal of havoc" (Bennett and White 2015: 74–75, emphasis added). In contrast, a blogger for NORML evaluated Colorado's policy after its first six months far more positively: "This policy has not only failed to cause the reefer madness social breakdown predicted by prohibitionists, it appears that this new industry is starting to positively impact the state and its communities" (Fendrick 2014). Thus, popularity and hazardousness remain central to the evolving policy debate.

Similarly, opposition to gun control is fueled by warnings that any reform will lead down a slippery slope toward the abolition of guns. (Chapter 4 discusses slippery-slope arguments in more detail.) Gun control advocates play into the opponents' narrative, not only by sometimes suggesting that eventually eliminating— or at least dramatically restricting—gun ownership is their goal, but also by pointing to other countries that have much more stringent limits on gun ownership, and by trying to institute bans against particular types of guns (such as Saturday night specials, all handguns, assault rifles, and .50 caliber rifles).* In contrast, polls show widespread support, even among gun owners and members of the National Rifle Association, for tighter regulations regarding background checks (Public Policy Polling 2015; Swift 2015). Thus, debates over both existing and prospective policies emphasize issues of popularity and hazardousness.

The Importance of Rhetorical Similarities

I've compared claims by individuals who oppose legalizing marijuana with those calling for tougher gun control policies in order to show rhetorical similarities: both use troubling typifying examples to illustrate harms; both emphasize the special vulnerability of the young to harm; and so on. A moment's thought reveals that arguments opposing all sorts of popular hazards can be—and are—constructed in analogous ways. Thus, protecting the vulnerable young figures into all sorts of claims about the dangers of pit bulls, tobacco, alcohol, automobiles, bicycles, the

---

* For decades, sociological analysts who have examined gun issues—many of whom have reported their personal histories of having opposed guns— have concluded that guns' popularity makes eliminating guns an impractical goal (Jacobs 2002; Wright, Rossi, and Daly 1983).

Internet, and other popular hazards. Such reasoning is culturally resonant: it draws from idealized, romanticized visions of childhood and youth as life stages characterized by innocence and vulnerability, overlaid with biomedicalized claims about the inability of immature brains to properly assess risks.

Advocates' claims are inevitably selective, in that they choose to emphasize lines of reasoning that seem to support their conclusions, even as they downplay or ignore arguments that might call those conclusions into question. As a result, debates over social policies toward popular hazards tend to feature proponents and opponents talking past one another, with the former emphasizing popularity, and opponents highlighting hazardousness.

This leads those who oppose various popular hazards to draw on parallel arguments, even when very different political realities confront the issues they address. Thus, firearms currently are subject to a fairly limited regulatory structure that gun control advocates seek to expand, while federal and most states' laws banning marijuana are under attack by those seeking to legalize the drug's recreational use. Guns are generally legal and marijuana is generally illegal; guns' opponents call for tougher regulations, while marijuana's opponents want to maintain the laws that exist. Yet, however different the two causes and their political contexts may seem, opponents of both popular hazards make parallel arguments in their efforts to persuade the public and policy makers. And, as noted earlier, the same sorts of similarities can be found in the claims of proponents of different popular hazards.

In sum, debates over popular hazards tend to revolve around differing assessments of their popularity and their hazardousness. Identifying popular hazards as an analytic category helps us identify parallels in the ways people talk about what are usually understood to be unrelated, even completely different, issues. This is important, because it has the potential to guide thinking about social policy.

DISCUSSION

Sociological analyses of social problems and social policies, like the claims made by advocates, tend to be issue-specific. That is, sociologists usually collect and analyze data from particularistic case studies-—focused on a particular problem or even particular aspects of that problem, perhaps at some specific time or place. They may, however, generalize and make broader statements about that problem—or about limited aspects of it—in other times and places (Best 2015). They are less likely to consider parallels across different social problems, such as the similarities in the rhetoric used by advocates of gun control and opponents of legalizing recreational marijuana use.

While issue-specific case studies have advantages, they also have limitations. Specifically, it is easy to get caught up in particulars and miss larger patterns. Popular hazards—a seemingly diverse range of activities—share two important features: they are very common, and they pose real risks. However, what are defined as the policy implications of these risks differ wildly across time and space. Credit cards are not seen as especially problematic, while cars, alcohol, and tobacco are subject to elaborate regulatory apparatuses. Swimming pools and bicycles, once largely unregulated, are increasingly subject to regulations designed to minimize risks. While some people continue to find pornography troubling, its spread to the Internet poses seemingly insurmountable challenges to would-be regulators. Appropriate policies toward other issues—such as marijuana legalization and gun control—continue to be hotly debated. Although it is easy to get caught up in the apparent differences among all of these issues, it is also important to appreciate the common underlying dilemma that they pose. That is, they all involve many people and, as a practical matter, will harm some of them: a society with lots of cars will have traffic accidents; a society with widespread alcohol consumption will have lives damaged by drinking; and a society with many firearms will have people struck by bullets.

The parallels among popular hazards have consequences. In spite of their apparent differences, the structural similarities among different issues tend to shape the terms of debate, to evoke some of the same rhetorical themes. Within the larger culture, topics such as freedom or the vulnerability of the young tend to resonate. Even though not everyone favors the same policies across all popular hazards, there will still be similarities in what is being debated across issues. This means that disagreements about, say, whether individual freedom or minimizing harm should be the central concern in shaping policy are likely to appear in arguments about many popular hazards. Yet individuals may be proponents of one popular hazard while opposed to another, even though the underlying issues are similar.

Policy debates over popular hazards sometimes include proposals to ban them. This is impractical. Their popularity makes it likely that forbidden popular hazards will simply go underground. There is a vast literature on the underground markets that emerge in the face of prohibitions against alcohol, gambling, illicit drugs, pornography, and the like. Such prohibitions always involve trade-offs. On the one hand, prohibiting a popular hazard is likely to reduce the number of people using the forbidden good or service: consumption of alcohol did decline during Prohibition, and no doubt fewer people placed bets when gambling was generally illegal. However, there are also costs: underground markets feature an unregulated and sometimes violent illicit trade; efforts to enforce the ban may lead to official corruption; and so on. Enforcing prohibitions tends to be both expensive and inefficient.

More effective social policies strive toward harm reduction. This tends to be a gradual process. The decline in traffic fatalities is the product of a long series of incremental reforms to promote safer drivers in safer cars on safer roads, just as the decline in tobacco smoking reflects policies to better educate people about the risks of smoking, to raise the cost of tobacco, and to restrict the number of places where people can smoke.

Policy choices are inevitably shaped by social context, including the political resources of proponents for different policies, the current cultural constructions of the hazard in question, and evaluations of existing policies. All of these contextual elements have histories: how today's options are understood is always shaped by what happened yesterday. Similarly, advocates may make comparisons with how societies in other times or places addressed the popular hazard under consideration. But it is far less common for people to acknowledge the underlying parallels among diverse popular hazards.

All popular hazards are hazardous. While it may be possible to imagine an ideal society in which there are no harms caused by tobacco, or marijuana, or cars, or guns, we do not live in that world. As a practical matter, all popular hazards have constituencies, and they all carry risks. Ignoring their underlying similarities leads to demonizing the risks posed by some popular hazards while excusing the harms caused by other hazards. This promotes rancor, rather than rationality. Acknowledging popular hazards' parallels is an important step toward devising social policies that actually minimize harms.

CHAPTER TWO

American Nightmares; or, Why Sociologists Hate the American Dream

WRITTEN WITH DAVID SCHWEINGRUBER

Consider some passages from recent textbooks for introductory sociology courses:

> Ask almost anyone about the American Dream and they are likely to mention some of the following: owning your own home; having a good marriage and great kids; finding a good job that you enjoy; being able to afford nice vacations; having a big-screen TV, nice clothes, or season tickets to your team's home games. For most Americans, the dream also means that all people, no matter how humble their beginnings, can succeed in whatever they set out to do if they work hard enough. In other words, a poor boy or girl could grow up to become president of the United States, an astronaut, a professional basketball player, a captain of industry, or a movie star (Ferris and Stein 2016: 206).

> "The American Dream" can mean many things. Sociologically, it refers to children being able to pass their parents as they climb the social class ladder (Henslin 2014: 274).

In the United States, the major ideology that justifies inequality is the American Dream. This ideology proposes that equality of opportunity exists in the United States and that anyone who works hard enough will get ahead. Conversely, anyone who does not succeed must be responsible for his or her own failures (Brinkerhoff et al. 2011: 163).

Clearly, these textbooks characterize the American Dream in different ways, sometimes within a couple of sentences. Is the American Dream attaining a secure, comfortable life (owning your home, having a good marriage and a good job), or does it involve reaching some pinnacle of achievement (the presidency or movie stardom)? Does it require intergenerational upward mobility? Does it imply that everyone has equal opportunities, or even that everyone can succeed?

Many textbooks adopt worried tones when they mention the American Dream. Ferris and Stein (2016: 206) note, "Oprah Winfrey's meteoric rise from a childhood of poverty to her position as one of the most powerful celebrities in American is often cited as a prime example of the American Dream. How does Oprah's success represent the exception rather than the rule?" But Andersen and Taylor (2011: 191) cast doubt even on more modest ambitions: "The American Dream of owning a home, a new car, taking annual vacations, and sending one's children to good schools—not to mention saving for a comfortable retirement—is increasingly unattainable for many," although Brinkerhoff and colleagues (2011: 163) concede that "the American Dream is, for some, a reality," and Hughes and Kroehler (2008: 199) explain that "the American Dream is a different reality depending on one's gender, race, and ethnicity." Henslin (2014: 274) is somewhat more optimistic: "The American Dream might be ailing, but it is still vibrant," a sentiment echoed by Macionis (2009: 316): "Even today, for some people at least, the American dream is alive and well." David Newman (2017: 319) observes that poverty is "people coming up short in their quest for the American Dream"; in an earlier edition, he warned, "Not surprisingly, many young people today feel that the American Dream is unattainable, at least for them" (2000: 505).

Not all introductory sociology textbooks mention the American Dream, but those that do conceptualize it in very different terms. For the most part, their treatments of the topic are critical, even suspicious. Newman (2017: 287) uses it to illustrate the concept of false consciousness ("As long as large numbers of poor people continue to believe ... [in the American dream,] resentment and animosity toward the rich will be minimized and people will perceive the inequalities as fair and deserved"). Others imply that the American Dream is diminished, no longer what it once was (e.g., Macionis's [2009: 316] heading: "The American Dream: Still a Reality?").

The confused, ambivalent treatment of the American Dream in textbooks reflects sociology's larger discomfort with the concept; articles and monographs within the discipline also reveal a critical, even hostile orientation toward the idea. But this is not entirely sociologists' fault. From its very origins, the concept of the American Dream has been not just confused but deeply ambivalent—simultaneously nostalgic and critical. Understanding the term's history can help us place the sociologists' discomfort in context.

THE ORIGINS OF THE TERM *AMERICAN DREAM*

Ask who coined the term *American Dream,* and you'll elicit a range of interesting guesses from deep in American history—

Abraham Lincoln, Andrew Jackson, even Benjamin Franklin. The correct answer is disappointing: James Truslow Adams.*

Now forgotten, Adams was a popular historian during the 1920s and 1930s. In 1931, he published an interpretive history of the United States, *The Epic of America* (Adams [1931] 1941), after his publisher rejected his proposed title—*The American Dream*—as too fantastic to attract Depression-era book buyers (Cullen 2003). Adams expounded on the concept in the book's epilogue:

> The *American dream,* that dream of a land in which life should be better and richer and fuller for every man, with opportunity for each according to his ability and achievement.... It is not a dream of motor cars and high wages merely, but a dream of a social order in which each man and each woman shall be able to attain to the fullest stature of which they are innately capable, and be recognized by others for what they are, regardless of the fortuitous circumstances of birth or position.... And that dream has been realized more fully in actual life here than anywhere else, though very imperfectly even among ourselves. (Adams [1931] 1941: 404–5)

In the next several pages, he worried about the threats to the "quality of thought" and "abiding values" posed by inequality, materialism, and popular culture before warning, "We have a long and arduous road to travel if we are to realize our American dream in the life of our nation" (p. 416).

It is important to appreciate Adams's cautious tone. He was not making complacent—let alone bombastic—claims about American society, nor was he oblivious or indifferent to inequality. Rather, he saw the American Dream as a widely shared

---

* Although Cullen (2003) and Samuel (2012) credit Adams with originating the term, lexicographers have found instances of the term's use at the beginning of the twentieth century (Stamper 2017).

ideal, as a goal toward which Americans should strive. He also expressed concerns that consumerism and materialism might lead Americans astray, that they could lose sight of the American Dream.

THE IMPERILED AMERICAN DREAM AS A RHETORICAL DEVICE

The concept of the American Dream was catchy and proved to have legs. It remains a rhetorical touchstone, a shorthand way for politicians, intellectuals, journalists, and all manner of other commentators to assess—and usually to raise concerns about—the state of American society. In fact, figure 3, which tracks the term's appearances in books published since 1920, reveals that its popularity has only increased over time.

The American Dream is rarely invoked in smug, complacent tones. Rather, consistent with the way Adams framed the concept, it is usually coupled with warnings about the once-robust Dream becoming endangered. For instance, the first time an American president explicitly referred to the American Dream appears to have been in 1937 (only six years after Adams published his book), when Franklin D. Roosevelt (1937) told Congress: "The American dream of the family-size farm, owned by the family which operates it, has become more and more remote." We can find parallel reasoning in hundreds of statements by later presidents, such as in a 2014 message to Congress from Barack Obama: "Too many young people entering the workforce today will see the American Dream as an empty promise—unless we do more to make sure hard work pays off for every single American" (Obama 2014).

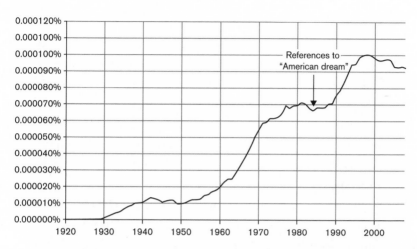

Figure 3. Ngram analysis of references to "American dream" in Google Books in American English, 1920–2010. Source: http://books.google.com/ngrams.

There are many other examples of politicians warning that the American Dream is endangered. For example, during the long campaigns for the 2016 Republican and Democratic presidential nominations, virtually every candidate used the theme. When Donald Trump announced his candidacy, he declared, "Sadly, the American dream is dead. But if I get elected president I will bring it back bigger and better and stronger than ever before, and we will make America great again" (Trump 2015). Similarly, Senator Ted Cruz warned, "The central challenge facing this country right now is that for millions of Americans, the American dream seems to be slipping away" (Mora 2015). Senator Marco Rubio, who had published a book titled *American Dreams* to accompany his campaign, also worried: "Here in America, anyone who works hard can leave their children better off than themselves. That is the real American Dream. But today, it is dying" (Peters 2016). Among the Democrats, Senator Bernie Sanders (2015) adopted similarly concerned rhetoric: "In the 1950s and 1960s, it was possible to graduate from high school and move right into a decent-paying job with good benefits.... A couple with a sole breadwinner could buy a home, raise a family and send their kids to college. That was the American dream. Unfortunately, today, for too many Americans, it's not a possibility." And Hillary Clinton (2016) promised to "do everything I can ... to restore the belief that, yes, the American Dream is alive."

But it's not just politicians who speak of the Dream. A *Time* magazine cover story warns, "The American Dream may be slipping away" (Meacham 2012: 32). The term is invoked in think-tank reports with titles such as *Generations in Pursuit of the American Dream* (Howe 2014), *Is the American Dream Alive?* (Bowman, Marsico, and Sims 2014), and *Pursuing the American Dream* (Pew Charitable Trusts 2012). Invoking the endangered American Dream is a conventional rhetorical device for commanding attention by warning that things seem to be bad or getting worse or about to start getting worse.

In sum, politicians and other commentators often warn that the American Dream in endangered. Presumably, threatened or diminishing opportunities should translate into public anxiety, skepticism, or even cynicism about the ideal of the American Dream. But what do public opinion polls show? In 2014, during the slow recovery from the Great Recession, an extensive review of poll results that addressed various aspects of the American Dream concluded the following (Bowman, Marsico, and Sims 2014: 2; cf. Hanson and Zogby 2010):

- Americans, by and large, believe that they can achieve their own version of the American Dream, and it is a personal vision. This view has changed little over the past 30 years. While a small group of skeptics exists, the average American believes that this is still a country of opportunity where personal success—material or otherwise—can be achieved with hard work and a little bit of ingenuity.

- People think the challenges to achieving the dream are greater than in the past.

- The key elements of the dream—an education for oneself and one's children and freedom to live life on one's own terms— still rank much higher in terms of priority than becoming wealthy.

- Americans continue to be more confident about their own children's prospects for achieving the American Dream than they are about the prospects of children overall.

- In 1986, whites were more optimistic than nonwhites about the American Dream. Today, whites in some polls are less confident than blacks and Hispanics about being able to achieve selected aspects of the American Dream.

In other words, public confidence in the American Dream remains fairly robust.

Because the American Dream lacks a precise definition, warnings about its imperiled status can tap into a variety of different themes. Politicians' rhetoric invoking the American Dream—much like the varied claims in introductory sociology textbooks—treat the concept as malleable, one that can be linked to all sorts of issues, from the availability of family farms to young people's job prospects. Often, it is invoked nostalgically, in claims that while the American Dream once was a realistic prospect, formerly available opportunities are no longer accessible, with unspecified social changes somehow to blame for the decline of the American Dream. Sometimes the term is equated with tremendous success (as when Oprah Winfrey is presented as an example); in other cases, it is understood in more modest terms (such as homeownership, something nearly 90 percent of Americans experience at some point in their adult lives [Rank, Hirschl, and Foster 2014]). It can refer to individuals advancing in their own lifetimes, or it can be understood to involve intergenerational mobility. The American Dream is almost always presented as universalistic—opportunities for improvement that are available to all—but some commentators couple that universalism with an ideal of equality, implying that the American Dream involves everyone having *equal* opportunities. Precisely because it is a common yet vaguely defined concept—a familiar cultural resource—it is easy to overlook these differences, to assume that everyone attaches essentially the same meaning to the American Dream.

This confusion has characterized the ways sociologists have incorporated the American Dream, not just in introductory textbooks aimed at first-year college students, but also in the books and articles aimed at their colleagues. Sociologists often have been critical of—-even seemed outraged by—the American Dream.

TRACING THE AMERICAN DREAM IN SOCIOLOGICAL WORKS

The standard trope about the threatened American Dream is echoed in sociologists' writings: "We cannot escape the realization that the American Dream hangs from a thread more slender and tenuous than ever before" (Hertz 2010: 653). However, these critiques rarely incorporate the concept directly in their analyses, if only because there is no clear, general agreement about just what the American Dream means.

One of the first major social scientists to comment on the concept, W. Lloyd Warner,* began his *Social Class in America* ([1949] 1960) by explicitly addressing the American Dream:

> When some men learn that *all* the American Dream does not fit *all* that is true about the realities of our life, they denounce the Dream and deny the truth of *any* of it. Fortunately, most of us are wiser and better adjusted to social reality; we recognize that, though it is called a Dream and though some of it is false, by virtue of our firm belief in it we have made some of it true.... Many Americans by their own success have learned that, for them, enough of the Dream is true to make all of it real. (3–4, emphases in original)

Here Warner taps into sociological ambivalence about the concept—should it be viewed as an idealized myth or as a flawed portrait of reality?

More recent analyses argue that belief in the American Dream varies among particular sectors of society. Thus, "workers who have been laid off, downsized, outsourced, and in some sense used as lubricant for the new market-sensitive flexible economy have greater pessimism concerning the American Dream than more privileged workers" (Starks 2003: 220), whereas "the results of our analysis underscore the importance of [the election of Barack Obama and other] symbols of black progress in altering blacks' perceptions of the American Dream" (Stout and Le 2012: 1350).

---

* Some sociological discussions link the American Dream to Merton's (1938) "Social Structure and Anomie," but that essay, which talks about "the extreme emphasis upon the accumulation of wealth as a symbol of success in our own society" (p. 675), does not use the term, which was not yet in wide circulation.

Books That Mention the American Dream
in Their Titles

By the end of 2015, sociology's two leading journals that publish book reviews—*Contemporary Sociology* (the *American Sociological Review* through 1971) and the *American Journal of Sociology*—had carried reviews of 47 books that mentioned the American Dream in their titles. Titles that invoked the American Dream became much more common over time; the 1950s and 1960s each saw only one such book reviewed, whereas there were 3 such titles reviewed in the 1970s, 9 in the 1980s, 15 in the 1990s, 12 between 2000 and 2009, and 6 between 2010 and 2015.

The first sociological book with *American Dream* in the title, Ely Chinoy's *Automobile Workers and the American Dream* (1955), used the concept in a way that would become familiar: contrasting the ideal of the American Dream with the actual experience of some group of people having difficulty achieving it. His book is "an attempt to explore how [autoworkers] live out their versions of the American dream in a world in which there is a palpable disparity between their experience and the prevalent myth" (p. 1). Sixty years later, a parallel analysis was subtitled *Trucking and the Decline of the American Dream* (Viscelli 2016).

Some later authors are much more scathing. In Jhally and Lewis's (1992) critique of *The Cosby Show*, the American Dream "offers wealthier citizens the comfort and satisfaction of feeling included but forces poorer people to denigrate their own lot, and ultimately, to denigrate themselves for having failed" (p. 75–76). "The American dream," they conclude, "is insidious, not innocent" (p. 139). Sieber (2005), who recasts the American

Dream as the American Myth, claims that this myth is "the most destructive element in our culture today because it blinds us to the perils of domestic and international backwardness and lends support to leaders who contribute to our inferiority of commission or omission" (p. 13). He warns that "casting aside the crutches of a Myth that prevent us from standing on our own feet and advancing with the strength of unflinching self-knowledge is a task that is by no means easy for a proud nation to undertake" (p. 311).

The titles of many other books adopt similarly worried, even alarmed, tones: *Awakening from the American Dream* (Miles 1976); *Rescuing the American Dream* (Goetze 1983); *Prisoners of the American Dream* (Davis 1986); *Persistent Poverty: The American Dream Turned Nightmare* (Ropers 1991); *Declining Fortunes: The Withering of the American Dream* (K. Newman 1993); *Poor Richard's Principle: Recovering the American Dream through the Moral Dimension of Work, Business, and Money* (Wuthnow 1996); *Illusions of Opportunity: The American Dream in Question* (Schwarz 1997); *Race, Self-Employment and Upward Mobility: An Illusive American Dream* (Bates 1997); *Bait and Switch: The (Futile) Pursuit of the American Dream* (Ehrenreich 2005); *Tensions in the American Dream: Rhetoric, Reverie, or Reality* (Bush and Bush 2015); and *A Dream Denied: Incarceration, Recidivism, and Young Minority Men in America* (Soyer 2016). Such titles mirror the introductory sociology texts' skeptical, critical treatment of the concept.

INDICTING THE AMERICAN DREAM

Sociologists' critiques of the American Dream take several forms. It may help to distinguish some of their arguments.

The American Dream Is a Myth

Well, yes. As the term suggests, the American Dream refers to aspirations, ideals, possibilities, opportunities, a vision of what could be, should be—a brighter future for the individual or for next generation. There is a reason why it isn't called the American Reality.

Myth is often treated in popular discourse as a pejorative— "That's just a myth" (meaning "That's false"). But it can have a very different meaning for sociologists; from Durkheim onward, we have understood that myths are sources of social solidarity, expressions of shared values.* Thus, we recognize the principle articulated in the Declaration of Independence that "all men are created equal" as a myth: while it has always been possible to make arguments that reality falls short of the ideal of equality, people continue to quote that principle and invoke it as a goal, to insist that it is a belief that ought to guide Americans' actions.

More often, instead of simply dismissing the American Dream as a myth, sociologists highlight the ways that social arrangements fall short of some ideal and then argue that these shortcomings call the validity of the American Dream into question. Consider five of these critiques, discussed below.

Not Everyone Is Upwardly Mobile

This is of course true. It is possible to frame this argument in extreme terms. Recall that Ferris and Stein's (2016: 206) textbook made the point that "Oprah's success represent[s] the exception rather than the rule." How can anyone argue?

---

* This usage is sometimes debased by sociologists who use terms such as *rape myths* or *disaster myths* to discredit claims they mean to attack as false.

Oprah Winfrey is a billionaire; in 2015, *Forbes.com* (2015) listed the four hundred richest Americans and ranked her $3-billion fortune in 211th place. Ferris and Stein also note that Oprah grew up in poverty. Currently, it is estimated that more than 16 million children live in poor households (National Center for Children in Poverty 2014). Obviously, they can't all make the Forbes 400 list of the richest Americans; perhaps less obviously, if Oprah distributed her entire fortune equally among poor children, each would receive less than $190. Certainly Oprah is an exception, an extreme outlier—but so what? If relatively few poor people become billionaires (a mathematical certainty), is that proof that something is seriously wrong with the American Dream?

What does it mean to get ahead? Think back to the early twentieth century, a time when life expectancies were about thirty years shorter than they are today; when only a small minority of young people graduated from high school and only a tiny percentage completed college; when fewer people owned their homes and large percentages of the places where people lived lacked indoor plumbing, electricity, or telephones (air-conditioning was virtually unheard of); when only a minority of people owned cars; and so on (cf. Leon 2016). A bit more than a century later, a substantial majority of Americans—including even the poorest Americans—live longer, vastly more comfortable lives (Rector and Sheffield 2011). When most people compare their lives to those of their parents or grandparents, they can see that things have improved. A 2012 study by the Pew Charitable Trusts (2012) found: "Eighty-four percent of Americans have higher family incomes than their parents had at the same age[;] and across all levels of the income distribution, this generation is doing better than the one that came before it"

(p. 5).* It is easy to imagine that, if the comparison stretched back to grandparents' or great-grandparents' generations, an even larger percentage would show improvements. Regardless of whether they're on a list of the wealthiest Americans, if those people think of the American Dream as measured in *absolute* terms—in terms of achieving a longer life expectancy, a higher level of education, and a higher standard of living—most people might reasonably conclude that they have indeed achieved the American Dream.

A large body of social scientific research seeks to measure social mobility. In earlier decades, researchers sought to identify the rate at which sons of blue-collar fathers moved up to white-collar careers (cf. Lipset and Bendix 1959). This is, of course, another absolute standard: every person who crosses the blue-collar/white-collar divide is defined as upwardly mobile. However, in recent decades, many analysts have chosen to measure mobility in *relative* terms. Often, they use quintiles: dividing the population into fifths along some dimension of wealth or income,

---

* Some economists worry that this sort of intergenerational progress is slowing:

> The American dream is that each generation should live twice as well as the previous one, and this requires that incomes rise at an annual rate of around 2 percent per year. At this pace, incomes will double every 35 years. Between 1947 and 1970, average real compensation in the US increased at annual rate of 2.6 percent—a pace that was actually faster than required to achieve the dream. But since 1970, the average real compensation of US workers has grown at less than 1 percent per year, and at that pace it would take almost a lifetime to see incomes double. (Lawrence 2016: 42)

Chetty et al. (2016) present evidence that barely half of American thirty-year-olds have higher incomes than their parents at the same age (down from over 90 percent in the early 1970s). This report attracted various critiques suggesting that it exaggerated the decline in absolute mobility rates (Winship 2016).

from the highest quintile to the lowest. Viewed in relative terms, someone who grew up in a second-quintile household, and whose adult life is spent in the second quintile has not been socially mobile and has not experienced the American Dream, no matter whether that person's life has improved according to absolute measures of life expectancy, education, or standard of living.

It is important to appreciate that measuring mobility in terms of changing quintiles or some other relative index of mobility assumes a zero-sum game. By definition, only a fifth of people occupy the highest quintile; for every person who rises to a higher quintile, there must be someone who falls into a lower one.* If we define achieving the American Dream in absolute terms—if, for instance, we say that it can be attained by anyone who achieves certain goals, such as homeownership or longer life expectancy or a certain standard of living—then the American Dream may be an experience shared by many people. But, if we insist on using some relative standard, such as gaining a position in a higher quintile, then winners can never outnumber losers.

The authors of introductory sociology textbooks seem to emphasize structural obstacles to upward social mobility as a way of debunking the broader culture's cheerful assumptions about America as a boundless land of opportunity. In this portrait, people who aspire to improve their lot find themselves frustrated, stuck, trapped, blocked, unable to get ahead. This story emphasizes the half-empty glass.

---

* This is not strictly true, because income quintiles refer to households, rather than individuals, and so the populations of quintiles vary: there are considerably more people in the top quintile (where households tend to be composed of married couples, often with two wage-earners) than in the bottom quintile. According to the 2015 *Current Population Survey*, 74.8 percent of the top- and 4.3 percent of the bottom-income-quintile households had two or more earners (Census Bureau 2016: table NIMC-05).

The data are somewhat more complicated: they hardly show that upward mobility from one generation to the next is nonexistent. The Pew study found that among those raised in bottom-quintile families, most—57 percent—reached a higher quintile as adults, while 43 percent remained "stuck" in the bottom quintile; among those who did rise, modest improvements from the fifth to fourth quintiles were more common (27 percent) than the most dramatic increases from the bottom quintile to the top (4 percent; Pew Charitable Trusts 2012). Those who had been raised in top-quintile families showed the reverse pattern—40 percent remained stuck in the top quintile, while only 8 percent fell all the way to the bottom quintile.*

Moreover, a substantial proportion of Americans experience fairly dramatic fluctuations in income over the course of their lives. Both ups and downs are common. Tracing the lives of adults between ages twenty-five and sixty, Rank, Hirschl, and Foster (2014: 99) found that "upward and downward income movement is very much part of the American economic landscape." Three-quarters of adults experienced at least one year of affluence (defined as an income exceeding one hundred thousand dollars), and nearly half experienced at least one year of near poverty (defined as income below 125 percent of the official poverty line). A parallel analysis using income tax records concluded, "There was considerable income mobility of individuals in the U.S. economy during the 1996–2005 period, and the degree of relative income

---

* Similarly, Reeves (2014b) found that among children raised in the bottom quintile, 36 percent remained stuck and only 10 percent reached the top quintile; while among top-quintile children, only 11 percent fell to the bottom quintile and 30 percent retained their positions at the top. This chapter relies on findings from three recent analyses of mobility: Pew Charitable Trusts (2012); Rank, Hirschl, and Foster (2014); and Reeves (2014b). The patterns in these results are reaffirmed by other studies.

mobility among income groups is roughly unchanged from the prior comparable period (1987–1996)" (Auten and Gee 2009: 328). The fluctuations in income both between generations and within an individual's biography challenge claims that social structure is too rigid and unchanging to allow much mobility.

Again, we are confronted with the choice between absolute and relative measures of mobility. No matter how much Americans' across-the-board standard of living improved in absolute terms, it is possible to argue that only individuals who moved to a higher quintile are upwardly mobile. Defining mobility in relative terms supports a view of social structure as rigid. This can lead to a somewhat peculiar definition of fairness: "[In] a perfectly mobile society, an opportunity utopia, being born ... in the bottom quintile would have no effect on where you ended up. You'd be equally likely to make it to the top as to stay at the bottom" (Reeves 2014a). That is, if a fair society is one in which one's starting quintile has no effect on where one winds up, then one-fifth of the children raised in bottom-quintile households in a fair society should wind up in each of the five quintiles (which, of course, they do not). Conversely, this would also mean that one-fifth of the children raised in top-quintile families should wind up in each quintile. In other words, using quintiles to measure mobility fosters a view that equates fairness with what are essentially random outcomes. Imagine a thought experiment in which we randomly assign each newborn an adult quintile. Would people actually view this as fair—or as chaotic?

Not Everyone Has an Equal Chance for Upward Mobility

In practice, most people do not assume that their children's prospects should be determined by some random process.

Richard V. Reeves, whose definition of a "perfectly mobile society" was quoted in the previous paragraph, concedes that "many of the mechanisms leading to the inheritance of status are legitimate, even laudable, such as committed and engaged parenting, an emphasis on education, and the transmission of productive values" (Reeves and Joo 2016). Parents try to steer their children toward favorable outcomes in their lives, and these efforts make a difference. However, these efforts run counter to "the rhetoric that all Americans have an equal chance at achieving the American Dream" (Rank, Hirschl, and Foster 2014: 161).* It is possible to improve children's outcomes, but the results do not produce an equality of random outcomes. The data reveal three factors that are especially important in shaping mobility prospects.

The first of these is *education*. Parents, teachers, and the larger culture all reinforce the message that it is important for young people to stay in school and to treat school seriously. There is a very strong correlation between educational attainment and income: on average, high school dropouts go on to earn less than those who graduate; those whose education ends at high-school graduation make less than those who begin some sort of postsecondary education; those who graduate from college have still higher incomes; and those who receive some sort of postbaccalaureate graduate or professional education earn still more. Public opinion polls consistently rank hard work and getting a good education as the most important factors in getting ahead in life (Bowman, Marsico, and Sims 2014). It is widely understood that most pathways to upward mobility and the American Dream run through schools.

* In fact, survey data show that Americans favor both having more children raised in the lowest quintile rise to the top, and allowing a substantial proportion of top-quintile children to retain their position (Davidai and Gilovich 2015).

Notice that a great deal of commonsense advice recognizes this pattern. Most children are bombarded with messages about the importance of education: they are urged to stay in school, study hard, and do as well as they can. The data confirm that this is good advice. Completing high school is important. Rank, Hirschl, and Foster's (2014: 128) data reveal that 55 percent of adults who completed high school experienced at least one year of affluence without ever experiencing near-poverty, compared to only 34 percent of those with less than a high-school education; similarly, 56 percent of those who did not complete high school experienced at least one year of near poverty without ever experiencing a year of affluence, compared to just 32 percent of those with more education.

Graduating from college also is important. The Pew study found that among those raised in bottom-quintile families, 47 percent of individuals who did not complete a college degree remained in the lowest quintile (while only 3 percent reached the top one; Pew Charitable Trusts 2012: 28). In comparison, among those raised in the bottom quintile but who completed college, only 10 percent remained stuck in the bottom quintile (and 10 percent rose to the top). Completing college also made a difference for those raised in the top quintile: among those who did not receive a college degree, 25 percent remained in the top, while 13 percent fell to the bottom quintile; but among college graduates 51 percent retained their top-quintile position, and only 4 percent dropped to the bottom.* As might be expected, it is easiest to

---

* Reeves (2014b) found that, among those raised in bottom-quintile homes who did not complete high school, 54 percent would remain in the bottom quintile, and only 5 percent would reach the top quintile; in contrast, among those who graduated from college, 16 percent remained stuck in the bottom quintile, while 20 percent rose to the top quintile.

move up or down one quintile, and hardest to shift between the top and bottom quintiles, but education improves children's upward mobility prospects in all quintiles. When adults encourage young people to stay in school, they're giving good advice.

In sum, education is widely understood to be the principal ladder for both intergenerational and intragenerational upward mobility. When people think of the American Dream, they think of opportunities that are available to those who work hard, who strive—and doing well in school is recognized as the earliest way, and one of the most important ways, that people can work hard to get ahead. The evidence shows that educational attainment—from a high school diploma to college graduation—boosts mobility prospects. Education may not completely level the playing field, but it makes opportunities more equal.

Second, *family structure* makes a difference. However unfashionable it may be to acknowledge this, children raised in households with two married parents are more likely to be upwardly mobile. Perhaps this is because these family units have more resources and can devote more attention to their children, or perhaps it is because the arrangement strikes the children as more stable and secure. Again, this pattern finds support in the larger culture's acknowledgment that it is "better for the children" for parents to stay married.

Consider children raised in bottom-quintile families. The chance of their remaining stuck in the bottom quintile when they are adults varies dramatically depending on their mothers' marital status: 50 percent of those with never-married mothers remain in the bottom quintile, versus 32 percent of those with mothers who were not continuously married and 17 percent of those whose mothers were continuously married (Reeves 2014b). And of course, family structure also affects bottom-quintile children's chances of reaching the top quintile: only 5 percent for those with never-married mothers, 10 percent for those whose mothers were not continuously married, but 19 percent for those with mothers who were continuously married (Reeves 2014b). Regardless of whether the parents are white, black, or Hispanic, or whether they are college educated or not college educated, family poverty rates are markedly lower when couples are married (Wilcox 2016).

In other words, family structure makes a difference in both children's and parents' prospects. Being married improves children's intergenerational mobility prospects, and couples who stay married are less likely to remain mired in poverty. This is a somewhat controversial claim—obviously marriage does not automatically transform people's economic standing, and no one would recommend remaining in a marriage characterized by brutality and violence. Moreover, many people are troubled by its implications for intergenerational mobility: is it fair to penalize individuals for the martial circumstances of their parents? Yet both liberal (Putnam 2015) and conservative (Murray 2012a) analysts agree: there is a marriage gap between upper-middle-class and poorer households. Upper-middle-class couples—who have more education and higher incomes—are more likely to marry, to postpone childbirth until they are married, and to stay married after they have children, while couples with less education and lower incomes are more likely to have children before marrying and to have those relationships dissolve. Those in the top quintile have advantages—marriage, more education, higher income—that reinforce one another.[*] However, parents in

---

[*] The 2015 *Current Population Survey* found that 16.5 percent of bottom-quintile households contained married couples, compared to 76.3 percent of top-quintile households (Census Bureau 2016: table NIMC-05).

lower-quintile households who manage to maintain their marriages and promote education boost the mobility prospects for their children.

Perhaps it is not marriage itself that boosts mobility prospects. Perhaps the ability to get and stay married reflects other desirable attributes, such as an ability to cooperate with others, Still, when young people are advised to imagine a future in which "you'll meet some nice person and settle down," that advice points toward a direct route to the American Dream.

The third factor is much more troubling: other things being equal, *race* continues to make a marked difference in individuals' chances for getting ahead. Data collected by Rank, Hirschl, and Foster (2014: 128) reveal that 44 percent of white adults experienced at least one year of affluence without ever experiencing near-poverty, compared to only 16 percent of nonwhites; similarly, 74 percent of nonwhites experienced at least one year of near poverty without ever experiencing a year of affluence, compared to just 40 percent of whites. Comparing blacks and whites born into bottom-quintile families, Reeves (2014b) found that 51 percent of blacks remain stuck in the bottom quintile, compared to only 23 percent of whites, while 16 percent of whites rose to the top quintile, compared to only 3 percent of blacks.* These are stark differences.

---

* The Pew Charitable Trusts (2012: 19) analysis has similar findings:

Blacks are more likely to be stuck in the bottom and more likely to fall from the middle of the family income and wealth ladders than are whites. A significant black-white gap also exists for relative mobility. More than half of black adults (53 percent for family income and 50 percent for family wealth) raised at the bottom remain stuck there as adults, but only a third of whites (33 percent for both) do. Blacks also are more downwardly mobile than whites. For family income, over half (56 percent) raised in the middle fall to the bottom or second rung as adults, compared with almost a third

Of course, race is conflated with other variables: whites have higher educational attainment than blacks, and they are more likely to be raised in families with married parents. We already know that education and family structure shape mobility chances; perhaps the apparent racial differences are largely explained by other factors. Thus, Haskins (2013) argues that children need to be taught that "they enter adulthood with three major responsibilities: at least finish high school, get a full-time job and wait until age 21 to get married and have children." However, critics respond, "among those who follow all three norms, blacks are significantly less likely to reach the middle class than whites who do the same. About 73 percent of whites who follow all three norms find themselves with income above 300 percent of the federal poverty line for their family size, while only 59 percent of blacks who adhere to all three norms fare equally well" (Gold, Rodrigue, Reeves 2015). Even among blacks who "play by the rules," the prospects for upward mobility are worse than for whites in similar circumstances.

The evidence that education, family structure, and especially race affect mobility prospects is important, particularly since individuals cannot be held accountable for race and their parents' marital status. Access to the American Dream is not distributed equally across society.*

(32 percent) of whites. For family wealth, more than two-thirds (68 percent) of blacks raised in the middle fall to the bottom or second rung as adults, compared with just under a third (30 percent) of whites.

* Another version of this critique notes that opportunities are especially constrained for those already in difficult circumstances. Two recent studies of incarcerated young men and factory workers who became unemployed after their plants closed argue that these populations are ill-served by belief in the American Dream: "The narrative of the 'American Dream' was so powerful because it distracted teenagers and juvenile justice workers alike from the

Americans Have No Better—and Actually Worse—Chances for Upward Mobility than People in Other Countries

This critique speaks directly to the question of American exceptionalism: is the United States different, in that it offers more opportunities for individuals to achieve upward mobility than other countries do? Many Americans simply take this as a given: of course we have more opportunities than people elsewhere. And yet the social scientific evidence often fails to confirm this widely held belief.

More than fifty years ago, Seymour Martin Lipset and Reinhard Bendix attempted to survey the literature on this question in *Social Mobility in Industrial Society* (1959). They concluded that "there is relatively little difference in rates of social mobility, as measured by the shift across the manual-nonmanual line, in countries for which sample survey data exist" (p. 72).*

There have been other, more recent efforts to measure social mobility rates across nations, using both absolute and relative mobility measures. Such studies face imposing methodological difficulties (Ganzeboom, Treiman, and Ultee 1991). However,

> while cross-country comparisons of relative mobility rely on data and methodologies that are far from perfect, a growing number of economic studies have found that the United States stands out as having less, not more, intergenerational mobility than do Canada

---

lack of real opportunities for change" (Soyer 2016: 10); "[the achievement ideology] focuses attention on how individuals, rather than the system, have failed, leading people to criticize others—and themselves—when they stay stuck in poverty and unemployment" (Chen 2015: 168).

* Note that Lipset and Bendix divided occupations into two categories—manual occupations (i.e., blue-collar, working with one's hands) and nonmanual occupations (i.e., white-collar, working with one's head). This is, of course, an absolute measure of mobility.

and several European countries. American children are more likely than other children to end up in the same place on the income distribution as their parents. Moreover, there is emerging evidence that mobility is particularly low for Americans born into families at the bottom of the earnings or income distribution. (Isaacs 2008: 6; cf. Beller and Hout 2006)

The United States more closely resembles other Western democracies in rates of intragenerational mobility: "Overall, American workers seem as likely as European workers to move up or down the earnings ladder in a 5- or 10-year period" (Isaacs 2008: 6).

In general, research results do not support claims of American exceptionalism: the United States seems to have more social mobility than some countries, but less than others. The discovery that mobility opportunities in the United States resemble those in Canada and western European countries runs counter to the ideology of the American Dream—or perhaps we should speak of a Canadian Dream, a Danish Dream, and so on.

Things Used to Be Better

Any of the above claims—not everyone is upwardly mobile, not everyone has an equal chance for upward mobility, and Americans aren't better at upward mobility than people in other countries—can be used to make nostalgic claims about social deterioration.

We have already noted how rhetorical uses of the American Dream tend to invoke threats. We are told our once-great nation used to be filled with opportunities, that ambitious, hardworking strivers could make something of themselves, but that things have gotten much tougher.

Such claims rely on selective memory. In many ways, American society in, say, 1900 was a hard world, one in a which people lived shorter lives, children received less education, the sick received less-competent medical care, and widows, orphans, and the disabled were forced to fend for themselves; yet in our rose-tinted imaginations, we envision this world as one of boundless opportunity. However, those rags-to-riches biographies of some great tycoons of the Gilded Age, such as Andrew Carnegie (a child of poor immigrants who started working in a factory yet went on to head U.S. Steel), were that era's equivalent of the Oprah Winfrey tale: stories of remarkably exceptional lives.

Social historians who have attempted to measure nineteenth-century mobility conclude that there were limits on both intra-generational and intergenerational mobility. Stephan Thernstrom (1964) pioneered the use of manuscript census schedules from the mid-nineteenth century to study social mobility; tracking males from one census to the next made it possible to see whether their occupational standing had improved (intra-generational mobility) and to identify fathers and their sons who shared households when the sons were young, which allowed him to measure intergenerational mobility. His case study found no rags-to-riches tales among unskilled laborers: "To practice the virtues exalted by the mobility creed rarely brought middle-class status to the laborer, or even to his children. But hard work and incessant economy did bring tangible rewards—money in the bank, a house to call his own, a new sense of security and dignity" (p. 164). These absolute improvements embodied the most common early American Dream experience.

Moreover, the United States has undergone structural changes since the mid-nineteenth century. In particular, access to education—and particularly higher education—became far more widespread, creating a ladder for upward mobility, and so "the direct link between social origins and destinations is severed among those men who attain a college degree" (Pfeffer and Hertel 2015: 164). The Horatio Alger hero—the shoeshine boy who through hard work and thrift becomes a tycoon—may be a figure of fantasy, but the poor child who stays in school, studies hard, and completes college has a good chance of attaining a middle- or upper-middle-class life.

There is a large literature that seeks to measure changing rates of mobility across American history, and which tends to get mired in debates over how to address structural changes—not just rising levels of educational attainment, but economic growth (which opens up more middle-class jobs), changes in family structure, farmers' declining share of the labor force, and so on—and debates over which decades offered more opportunities (Beller and Hout 2006).

There has always been some social mobility, but it has never been the case that everyone was socially mobile. The idea that opportunities were dramatically different in the past cannot be confirmed using the data available to social historians; but to the degree that there have been long-term changes, they have probably made American society more, not less, open to upward mobility.

The American Dream Can Be Equated with Individualism, Consumerism, or Materialism

This critique differs from the others in that instead of questioning whether Americans are able to achieve their goals, it suggests that their goals may not be worth pursuing. Sociologists have been warning about the demise of community and the threat of loneliness for decades, as evidenced by the titles of such classic works as *The Lonely Crowd, The Pursuit of Loneliness,* and *Bowling Alone.* These claims are often coupled with assertions about the meaningless pursuit of material goods. In many sociologists' views, individualism, consumerism, and materialism are signs of empty lives, and it is problematic that the American Dream encourages pursuing these things.

Of course, consumption of material goods shapes living standards, which in turn can be seen as a form of the American Dream. In a century, we've gone from being a society in which only a minority of homes had refrigerators, to one in which refrigeration is virtually ubiquitous. Presumably no one would truly argue that the spread of refrigerators is a serious social problem. Or consider personal computers, or cell phones, or smartphones—all perceived almost as luxury items when they first appeared, now viewed as near necessities. How can analysts decide which consumer goods are disturbing signs of consumerism?

When pollsters ask people what makes a good life, the public's responses focus on family, security, and good health; achieving wealth scores well down the list (Bowman, Marsico, and Sims 2014). Decades of surveys find that a substantial majority of Americans profess themselves relatively happy and satisfied (Best 2011b). They don't complain that they are lonely or wish they had more friends. And, while they are happy to shake their heads with concern over the future of the larger society, they express considerable confidence in their own and their children's prospects. Similarly, ethnographies of society's most marginal members consistently find that they are embedded in webs of supportive social ties. Sociologists may insist that large numbers of people live empty, alienated lives, but opinion polls suggest that many of those folks haven't figured that out.

SO WHY HATE THE AMERICAN DREAM?

The American Dream is best understood as a straw figure, designed for the expression of rhetorical ambivalence. The ideal of the American Dream celebrates American culture's potential strengths—openness and opportunity—at the same time that it acknowledges the ways reality falls short of the Dream. Even the term's originator, James Truslow Adams, devised it as a way of warning about what he saw as threats to the common culture—inequality, materialism, and a debased popular culture. And politicians of all stripes have worried that the American Dream is endangered. The American Dream is rarely invoked with complacency; it is almost always framed in terms of anxiety or critique.

Sociologists often seem blind to this subtlety: they seem to equate the American Dream with bombastic optimism that ignores the problems in American society. Further, they seem determined to demonstrate not just that reality falls short of the American Dream's idealism but also that the American Dream is a dangerous illusion—or perhaps delusion—because American society actually offers little openness or opportunity and presents lots of rigidity instead. They seem to delight in demolishing what was, after all, designed to be a straw figure.

The data are more mixed: if we define upward mobility in absolute terms involving life expectancy, educational attainment, and standard of living, it has been widespread; and even if we define it in relative terms, it is not uncommon (although Oprah-style, from-near-the-bottom-to-the-very-top mobility is necessarily rare). Sociologists express concern that opportunities vary depending on educational attainment, family structure, and race. Surely, they say, these inequities reveal that the American Dream is nothing more than an empty promise.

Sociologists' insistence on debunking the notion of the American Dream may be a product of changes within the discipline. Sociology has long been much more liberal and politically homogeneous than other scholarly fields.* In recent decades, this has been reflected in various developments, particularly sociologists' turn to an emphasis on inequality. Figure 4 offers one illustration of this tendency: it tracks the relative frequency of articles in the discipline's two leading journals, the *American Sociological Review* and the *American Journal of Sociology,* containing the words *equality* and *inequality* by graphing the number of articles mentioning inequality per article mentioning equality. Through the 1960s, the articles were about twice as likely to mention equality as inequality (i.e., for every two articles mentioning equality, there was about one mentioning inequality); but since the 1980s, articles mentioning inequality have outnumbered those mentioning equality. We can imagine that discussions of equality often refer to it as a value or the goal of some social movement; the word is likely to be used in a positive sense. In contrast, speaking of inequality is more likely to involve a critique of social structure or other social arrangements. The new focus on inequality is apparent in other ways. In many sociology departments, the social stratification course—long a staple offering—has been renamed "Social Inequality." Even if the old name is retained, many popular textbooks now have *Social Inequality* as their title, while other titles manage to incorporate both terms (e.g., *Social Stratification and Inequality, Introducing Social Stratification: The Causes and Consequences of Inequality,* and so on).

This focus on inequality heightens sociologists' suspicion of the American Dream. No doubt many introductory sociology

---

* For further discussion of this point, see chapter 6.

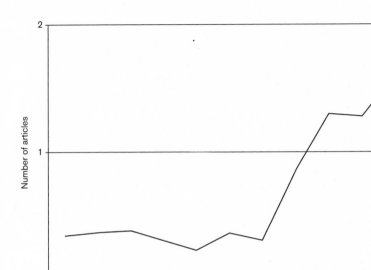

Figure 4. Number of articles in the *American Sociological Review* and the *American Journal of Sociology* that mention *inequality* per article mentioning *equality,* by decade, 1900–2009.

courses over the decades have used the American Dream to frame discussions of social mobility, as a way of encouraging students to think more critically about how American society is structured. No doubt sociologists have always treated the American Dream as a straw figure. But to the degree that the American Dream holds out the possibility of rising above social barriers, it can, given the discipline's current concerns, be seen as downplaying the importance of inequality, as challenging a theme that has become increasingly central in sociologists' thinking.

Given the state of the discipline, the American Dream seems like an obvious foil through which sociologists can communicate findings about stratification and mobility to undergraduates or the public. However, given some of the research summarized above, we could just as well start with some politicians' quotes about the death of the American Dream and then demonstrate that things aren't quite that bad—while still showing how social arrangements make upward mobility easer for some than others. Or we could start by contrasting the most optimistic and pessimistic accounts of the American Dream and then showing that the truth lies somewhere in between. The choice of the American Dream as a favorite straw figure says more about the obsessions of sociology than it does about the state of inequality in America.

There is no reason for sociologists to be surprised that social mobility is patterned, to discover that education improves mobility prospects and that opportunities are unevenly distributed across races. Identifying such patterns, measuring them, and trying to trace how they may be changing over time are fundamental forms of sociological analysis. The question is not whether the American Dream reflects some sort of universal reality—of course it does not. But outrage directed at the American Dream does nothing to help sociologists find the best way of framing our research for—or communicating our findings to—the public. Catharsis aside, expressing indignation while demolishing a straw figure has less value than exploring how social processes work.

PART TWO

Constructing Future Problems

Evaluating Predictions; or, How to Compare the Maya Calendar, Social Security, and Climate Change

Sociologists who study social problems tend to concentrate on the present, to focus on current problems in contemporary society. Less often, they turn their attention backward, to consider the history of particular social problems, usually in an effort to understand how we got to where we now are. However, sociologists tend to be wary of looking in the other direction, of peering into the future. Analyzing potential future social problems seems precarious, even to fall outside sociology's purview.

Still, claims about social problems often incorporate the future in their rhetoric. There are warnings about the devastating consequences of allowing some current trend to continue ("If we don't act now, things will soon get much worse"). (I have more to say about such language in the next chapter.) As we have seen, concerns about the American Dream often include such future talk ("Whereas once America was the land of opportunity, the future now seems bleak"). And sociological analysts often imply that some social problem is growing larger. Yet we rarely consider how claims about the future are rhetorically different from those about the present and the past.

All claims about the future are vulnerable to skepticism: How can anyone possibly know what the future holds, given that it is yet to unfold? It is arguably possible that any forecast about what is going to happen may be proven wrong. At the same time, social life depends on a sense of predictability; people need to be able to have expectations, to plan for the future. So there is an inevitable tension between our sense of uncertainty about what may happen, and our need for some confidence about what is going to come. Whenever people make claims about the future of social problems, this tension can come into play, with those who advocate action saying that unless we act, some problem will occur, and skeptics casting doubt on those predictions.

There are multiple ways to resolve this tension; not all future claims are treated as equal. They can be advanced by very different advocates, depend on very different sorts of reasoning, and inspire very different reactions. Warnings about what is going to happen are common; they compete for our attention and concern. In general, the most compelling claims are those supported by what their audiences judge to be *compelling evidence,* and which warn of *big problems* that are *quite likely to occur* in the *relatively near future* (Best 2011a). But of course not all future claims succeed; some are dismissed or ignored even as others arouse public concern and lead policy makers to act. What accounts for these different outcomes?

Let's compare three recent future claims that all predicted the likely arrival of a serious crisis in the near future. These claims were supported by very different sorts of evidence, and they evoked very different reactions. After examining each prediction in turn, we will ask what these cases can tell us about the nature of future claims.

THE MAYA CALENDAR AND THE PROJECTED END OF THE WORLD IN 2012

Our first case is perhaps a bit unfair, in that the prediction has already proven false. This was the claim that a calendar of the ancient Maya forecast that the world—or at least the world as we know it—would end on December 21, 2012. (Spoiler alert: this does not seem to have happened.) However, in the run-up to 2012, this particular claim received considerable attention. Although it is hard to know how many people actually took the Maya prophecy seriously, one international survey found that 2 percent of Americans strongly agreed and another 7 percent somewhat agreed with the statement "I have been experiencing anxiety or fear because the world is going to end in 2012" (Global @dvisor 2012). While the vast majority paid little attention, a small minority of people reported being at least somewhat concerned.

The claims about the Maya calendar prediction are an example of what we might call *time-certain warnings* about future catastrophes. That is, they forecast that a dramatic crisis will occur on or by a particular date. Social scientists have long been interested in such predictions because they pose an intriguing question: If some people believe in a very specific prediction—that, say, the world will end by a given date—and that prediction fails to come true, how will those folks deal with the realization that something they believed has proven to be false? This has led researchers to study various religious cults and other groups that have held such beliefs.* In general, the results of these studies tend to be anticlimactic: believers tend to shrug off any apparent contradiction when a prediction is not fulfilled and to devise explanations for why the failed prophecy need not threaten their other beliefs. Some groups of believers have tolerated even repeated failures of time-certain predictions.

There have been many, many such claims giving advance notice of the particular date upon which there will be some serious crisis. The Y2K concern, for instance, warned about terrible consequences of early computer programmers having conserved computer memory by using only two digits to record years, so that 1980 was recorded as "80" and 1981 as "81." While this convention may have made sense for early programs written when there was a premium on conserving even small amounts of computer memory, the arrival of the year 2000 was projected to cause problems, in that computers might not be able to recognize that "00" followed "99," and that this glitch might somehow interfere with the workings of computer programs. While most experts were skeptical, they acknowledged that contemporary society involves vast numbers of interlinked computer systems that depend on one another to function. Even if only some computers failed, the consequences could reverberate throughout modern society, as one popular guide for preparing for the crisis explained (Munch 1999: 2–3):

* The classic work on this subject is *When Prophecy Fails,* the 1956 study of a flying saucer cult that had announced aliens' impending destruction of earth (Festinger, Riecken, and Schachter 1956). Most studies of failed prophecies come from researchers on new religions and social movements (e.g., Zygmunt 1970); however, Farley (1998) examines concerns raised by a self-proclaimed climatologist's prediction of a major earthquake in 1990.

If many of the computers, software, and chips are not reset, fixed, or replaced correctly, some experts have predicted dire forecasts:

- Electrical systems may shut down in parts of the country....
- Our food supply (in grocery stores) may be interrupted because orders may not be correctly processed or shipped.
- Banks, stock brokerages, and insurance companies may not open....
- Ill-functioning computers may hamper branches and offices of our government....
- Some medical equipment may not function, either shutting off, operating incorrectly, or reporting inaccurate information.
- Computers may not function at all....
- Telephones, pagers and other tools of our communications system may not work.

In fact, governments and corporations took the Y2K threat seriously and undertook thorough, expensive reviews of their computer systems to insure that there would be no ill effects, so the predicted crisis did not occur (Quigley 2005).

Concern about Y2K depended on a story about potential technological failures. In that sense it was different from most time-certain forecasts of doom, which tend to be rooted in some sort of religious or mystical prophecy. Thus, in the run-up to 2012, radio evangelist Harold Camping received some media attention for predicting that Christ's Second Coming would be on May 21, 2011; when that failed to occur, he pushed the time-certain date back five months to October 21. Camping had a track record: beginning in the 1970s, he had made numerous, time-certain forecasts of the world's end. Following the failure of his October 21 prediction, he "conceded that he had been wrong about the timing and had no evidence that the world would end soon" (McFadden 2013). However, the long history of similarly failed religious prophecies has done little to discourage others from making similar claims.

The Maya calendar prediction derived from a New Age spiritual rereading of the stone carvings left by the ancient Maya, whose civilization seems to have collapsed in the ninth century. Carved calendars—presumably used for religious purposes—are part of the archeological record. One of these, sometimes called the Long Count calendar, measures time in *bak'tun*s, a unit of 144,000 days (one *bak'tun* lasts nearly four hundred years). Actually, this is a serious oversimplification, akin to saying that our calendar measures time in centuries. Just as we have both smaller units of time (such as months, years), and longer ones (such as millennia), so does the Long Count calendar (twenty *k'atuns* make up one *bak'tun,* twenty *bak'tun*s make one *piktun,* and so on; Stuart 2011: 237). The supposedly key date in 2012—generally agreed to be December 21—marked the end of the thirteenth *bak'tun*—a noticeable date, much as December 31, 1999, seemed noticeable. But, Y2K fears aside, people expected that December 31, 1999, would be followed by January 1, 2000. Similarly, the last day of the thirteenth *bak'tun* would ordinarily be followed by the first day of the fourteenth *bak'tun.* Still, having a time-certain date for the *bak'tun*'s end was inviting: it could be coupled to all manner of predicted futures.

So how did the coming end of the current *bak'tun* get equated with the end of the world? Professional archeologists and historians agree that millenarianism (the belief in some sort of dramatic, impending transformation in society) was not part of Maya culture, so it was unlikely that the Maya would have seen the *bak'tun*'s end as particularly significant (Restall and Solari 2011). But of course, millenarianism is an idea that runs through

Western culture (which is why we have all of those world-ending predictions). Enthusiasts linked all manner of futures to the *bak'tun*'s end, and these ranged from extremely pessimistic (the destruction of the world) to extremely optimistic (December 21 would signal the beginning of some new era of enhanced human consciousness).

Claims that something dramatic would occur in 2012 were bolstered by all sorts of evidence. Books promoting the idea featured dozens of illustrations of Maya glyphs and of star charts, all of them presented as evidence for the authors' claims (e.g., Argüelles 1987; Jenkins 2009). Of course, not everyone interpreted this evidence in the same way. Academic authorities (Restall and Solari 2011; Stuart 2011) dismissed the work of New Age enthusiasts, and vice versa. The New Age position drew on a classical mystical trope—the wisdom of the ancients—that insists that earlier civilizations understood the workings of the universe in important ways that are now forgotten. Often such claims have focused on the wisdom of ancient Egyptians, but the Maya—another pyramid-building culture—have been receiving increasing attention: "Maya teachings ... belong to a Perennial Philosophy, or Primordial Tradition, a reservoir of knowledge and spiritual wisdom common in its essential form to all great religious traditions.... [They] can speak to us today, or to any human being in any era" (Jenkins 2009: 8–9). Everyone credits the Maya with having developed a base-20 counting system and making careful observations of the night skies, but enthusiasts see larger meanings in these accomplishments. The notion that these ancients knew the secrets of the universe can be mixed and matched with all sorts of otherworldly ideas. Thus, José Argüelles (1987: 194) describes the run-up to 2012 as being "singularly directed to the emplacement of galactic synchronization crews at all the planetary light-body grid-nodes.... Then [as the *bak'tun* ends], as if a switch were being thrown, a great voltage will race through this finally synchronized and integrated circuit called humanity.... Like an iridescent rainbow, this circumpolar energy uniting the planetary antipodes will be instantaneously understood as the external projection of the unification of the collective mind of humanity."

But how and why, even if the *bak'tun*'s end did foretell some sort of cosmic transformation or catastrophe, might this come about—galactic synchronization crews aside? Enthusiasts claimed to find other evidence for the significance of 2012, most of it involving astronomical phenomena (Joseph 2007; Morrison 2009). Some noted that the cycle in sunspot activity would peak in 2012, which might produce massive solar flares with the potential to disrupt electronic communications on earth. Others forecast cataclysmic volcanic activity. Still others worried that the earth might collide with a large asteroid or with Nibiru—the brown planet that some New Age figures claim shares earth's orbit, but on the opposite side of the sun, where it has never been observed, which in 2012 would leap from its orbit and speed toward us. Or there would be a galactic alignment (when the centers of the earth, the sun, and the Milky Way galaxy would become arrayed as points along a single straight line). Or—but you get the idea. All sorts of notions that had little or nothing to do with the Maya could be connected to them by specifying 2012 as the date when something—something possibly of grand significance—was expected to happen. This offered a sort of symbiosis: ideas about, say, Nibiru's collision with earth could be assigned a date, even as claims about Nibiru, and so on, offered answers to the question "Why should we take the Maya calendar seriously?"

Of course, most serious people ignored the 2012 forecasts. The mainstream news media devoted little attention to the predictions (the fact that 2012 also featured a presidential election meant there was plenty of other news to cover). Popular culture displayed more interest: there was a big-budget disaster movie (*2012*—released in 2009); the Discovery and History cable channels ran several programs on the topic that stitched together dramatic footage of hurricanes and other disasters with clips of interviews with New Age experts, and there were countless books and webpages devoted to 2012, most of them directed at those sympathetic with various New Age beliefs. Occasionally scholars—specialists in Mesoamerican studies or astronomy—would step up to debunk some claims, but there is little evidence to suggest that large numbers of people got caught up in the concern. Few people seemed to expect the world to end on December 21, 2012, which did not make for dramatic news stories, and most news media gave these predictions the minimal, skeptical coverage usually allotted to preachers' time-certain forecasts of the Second Coming.

In short, the 2012 Maya calendar predictions attracted relatively little interest, and there is no evidence that they ever aroused much concern from policy makers. However, they offer a useful contrast with our other two predictions, which have received far more serious attention from the press, the public, and policy makers.

PROJECTIONS FOR THE SOCIAL SECURITY SYSTEM RUNNING OUT OF MONEY

Arcane spiritual reasoning both underpinned the Maya calendar prediction and explained why that belief attracted few adherents. We can contrast that now-failed prediction with forecasts that the Social Security system will run out of money in the foreseeable future. These predictions are based on relatively straightforward arithmetic calculations.

The U.S. Social Security system is funded by FICA (Federal Insurance Contributions Act) taxes and is supposed to operate independently of the rest of the federal budget (which is funded through federal income taxes and other revenue sources). In 2016 (when this book was written), taxpayers had 6.2 percent of their income withheld for Social Security taxes (matched by an equivalent amount paid by their employers); however, these taxes were collected only on the first $118,500 of annual income. This meant that individuals paid no additional Social Security taxes on earnings above that amount.

Many people seem to imagine that they have personal Social Security accounts to which they contribute, and from which they will later receive payments, and that the money they expect to receive after they retire is simply "their money." In fact, the vast majority of Social Security recipients receive far more from the program than they contributed to it. Nor is the money they receive somehow the same dollars that were withheld from their paychecks. Instead, money that is withheld this year basically goes to pay this year's recipients; the dollars that an individual can expect to receive in the future will come from withholding money from future workers' paychecks.

For decades, critics have warned that Social Security is actuarially unsound. That is, at some foreseeable point the payments promised in the future will inevitably exceed the funds that will have been collected. Typically, their forecasts point to the system failing sometime in the relatively near future. Thus, a 1956 book (*Social Security: Fact and Fancy*) warned, "This colossal enterprise is carried on with neither a plan to raise the money to pay for it, nor any realistic effort to relate what is promised to what will be or can be raised.... [U]nder its mounting costs, the whole system is sinking toward a collapse" (Stokes 1956: 100, 134). Fifteen years later, a similar volume with an even more strident title (*The Social Security Fraud*) insisted, "It is quite certain that compulsory Social Security taxes and benefits will be expanded as they have been right from the start" (Ellis 1971: 151). And thirty years later, another volume with another alarming title (*Social Security: False Consciousness and Crisis*) declared, "While Social Security can unquestionably meet its obligations to today's beneficiaries, and its financing is adequate for the short run, demographic forces doom the program in the longer term" (Attarian 2002: 6). In recent years, some conservative politicians and commentators even have characterized Social Security as a Ponzi or pyramid scheme.

These claims have left the public concerned; Gallup Polls taken over the past two decades have found that around half of nonretirees suspect they will not receive Social Security benefits (Newport 2015). Actually, few critics foresee the complete collapse of the system: "By law, Social Security cannot spend money it does not have. Therefore, if nothing is done before the trust fund reserves are exhausted in 2033, Social Security benefits would be cut by about 25 percent to match benefits going out with taxes coming in" (Ellis, Munnell, and Eschtruth 2014: 45).

Some even argue that the problem is illusionary: "The Social Security system has no chance of failing—never did and never will—therefore, it does not need to be 'saved.' ... The government has the power to tax, the ability to borrow, and it can use any source of funds available to pay Social Security benefits" (Santow and Santow 2005: 84). While this may be intended to reassure people, it ignores the point that future Social Security revenues will not be able to cover the program's costs, and that paying recipients what the government has promised to pay will require unpopular measures—some combination of massive borrowing, a large tax increase, or significant cuts in other federal programs so that dollars can be shifted to Social Security.

Obviously, the Social Security system has outlasted some of its earliest critics' predictions. What happened? Were these doomsday forecasts no more accurate than the Maya calendar prediction? No. We understand what's going to happen with Social Security quite well. We have a pretty good idea how many people will be eligible to collect Social Security next year, and the year after, and on into the future. We also have a good idea of how much they will have to be paid, and how much money will be collected in Social Security taxes. Forecasting Social Security's finances is basically a matter of arithmetic; there are no Social Security skeptics among people who understand the issue. People can look at the figures and agree on a rough date when the system is likely to run out of money.

Well, actually, it is more complicated than that. Forecasting Social Security's future can never be a matter of pinpoint accuracy. We have a pretty good idea of when the system is likely to run out of money, although the exact date inevitably depends upon contingencies. The number of workers paying FICA taxes may turn out to be somewhat higher or lower than projected (e.g., a major recession may reduce the number of people who are employed and paying taxes); the number of people receiving Social Security checks may prove to be higher or lower than projected (e.g., life expectancies may rise or fall faster than expected); cost-of-living increases may be higher or lower than anticipated; and so on. Moreover, the American population is continually changing in ways that affect the system. Are more women working? That means that there will be more people paying Social Security taxes. But if those women have fewer children on average, that means there will be fewer Social-Security-tax-paying workers in the future. And isn't life expectancy increasing? That means there will be more old people collecting even more monthly Social Security checks over the course of their lives. And will today's trends continue, or will they for some reason be reversed?

Such uncertainties make it if harder to predict exactly what is going to happen, and each year the Social Security Trustees release a report updating their forecast; the 2015 report warned that unless the program was modified, the trust fund would be depleted in 2034. In bad economic years, that horizon may be projected to be a year of two closer, just as it may recede a bit in boom years. Our confidence in these forecasts diminishes the further we peer into the future. Still, there is general agreement that maintaining the Social Security system poses challenges.

Debates about Social Security's future are not about the facts so much as about what should be done. When critics warn that the system will inevitably run out of money, they are arguing that the current arrangements are actuarially inadequate—and over the years the folks who made these arguments have been correct. Continuing to levy Social Security taxes at the current rates and paying benefits at the current level will indeed cause the system to run out of money. Similarly, when Social Security's defenders insist that the system is easily fixed, they are calling for changing those current arrangements. And in fact, Social Security has been "fixed" several times. (Histories of Social Security detail the various changes in its financing and coverage [Béland 2005; Schieber and Shoven 1999].)

There are two basic ways to fix Social Security. The first is to raise FICA taxes. There are various ways to do this, but two are especially important. The first is to raise the percentage of income withheld for Social Security. Since 1990, the rate has held steady at 12.4 percent. (That is, employees have had 6.2 percent withheld from their paychecks, and employers have paid another 6.2 percent to the federal government. While people are encouraged to think of this as a tax on employers, economists would argue that this is really a tax on employees, in that these expenses are part of the cost of labor.) In 1937, when the program started, the rate was only 2 percent, and it increased to 3 percent in 1950, 6 percent in 1960, 8.4 percent in 1969, and 10.16 percent in 1979—each increase generating more money that could be paid to beneficiaries. (Obviously, there must be an upper limit to these increases. It is not just that the FICA tax cannot exceed 100 percent of income. Would people be willing to have, say, 20 percent of their income withheld to pay the Social Security tax? Thirty percent?)

A second way to raise taxes is to increase the limit on taxable earnings. Individuals now pay FICA taxes on their first $118,500 in income, another figure that also has gone up dramatically since 1937, when it was $3,000. (Some advocates of this method argue that Social Security taxes should be collected on a much larger share—even all—of income. This is a politically attractive proposal because it affects only those earning more than $118,500—or whatever the current limit happens to be.) Obviously, taxing income at a higher rate or taxing a larger share of the income of those who make more money are two ways to generate more income for the Social Security program and thereby fix Social Security by increasing the funds available for benefits.

A second option is to reduce the amounts beneficiaries receive from Social Security. Again, this can be done in various ways. The most straightforward is to raise the age at which individuals can collect their Social Security checks. When the program began, the "normal" retirement age—the age at which one could begin to collect full benefits was sixty-five. Currently it is sixty-six and is scheduled to gradually increase to sixty-seven in 2026, which will save money by reducing the total amount paid to each individual recipient.

Another method of reducing benefits is to slow the rate at which benefits rise. Currently recipients receive cost-of-living increases that are gauged to the Consumer Price Index for Urban Wage Earners and Clerical Workers. Critics argue that this index actually exaggerates the amount of inflation because it ignores ways consumers adjust their behavior as prices change. They have suggested tying increases to the Chained Consumer Price Index for All Urban Consumers, which, they argue, gives a lower but more realistic vision of the cost of living, and which tends to rise more slowly (this would mean slightly lower annual cost-of-living increases).* Such alterations may not seem all that drastic, in that they propose modest cuts in each individual's benefits; but when multiplied by the tens of millions of people receiving Social Security checks, they add up to real savings. But of course, fixes that reduce benefits are unpopular because, by definition, they work to the disadvantage of at least some beneficiaries.

---

* Other critics call for indexing cost-of-living increases to the Experimental Consumer Price Index for Americans 62 Years of Age and Older, which gives more weight to "health care expenditures and other items whose prices tend to rise more rapidly" (Whittaker 2015: 1). This proposal would of course increase the program's costs by paying higher benefits.

So, there are lots of ways to prevent Social Security from running out of money. But if there are so many alternative solutions, why is the program's demise continually predicted? Very simply, none of the options are politically popular. Congress is reluctant to raise taxes, and the program's defenders—especially the 40-million-member AARP (formerly an abbreviation for the American Association of Retired Persons, now the organization's official name)—stand ready to denounce any plan to cut benefits. In recent years, proposals from Democrats to reform Social Security have tended to advocate generating more income for Social Security by raising the maximum for taxable earnings (which would mean higher taxes, but only for the relatively small proportion of the population that earns more than $118,500). Meanwhile, Republicans have called for privatizing parts of the program by allowing individuals to place some portion of the money now in their Social Security accounts in investment funds. This would have the advantage of reducing the government's obligation to cover some of the program's rising costs, and individuals' accounts could possibly gain greater value and pay higher benefits—but at the risk that the accounts' investments might lose money instead. Others have called for shifting benefits, so that lower-income recipients who rely heavily on Social Security receive more, while high-income recipients who are less dependent on the program receive less. All of these proposals encounter stiff opposition, which is why former House Speaker Tip O'Neill called Social Security the "third rail of American politics." The result is inertia, postponing action at least until the impending crisis seems much closer.

But there is another complicating issue. Even as people have worried about finding ways to prevent Social Security from running out of money, there have been calls to make coverage more just and, in the process, more generous. These involve advocates identifying categories of individuals who ought to be added to the program or whose benefits ought to be increased. This is not a new phenomenon. In 1957, *Time* ran a story titled "Social Security: The System Is Running in the Red" that argues, "Politicos of both parties have long been locked in a headlong competition to win votes by spreading Social Security coverage" (*Time* 1957: 72). Charles Murray (2012b) argues that this is a tendency of all entitlement programs and speaks of the "Law of Imperfect Selection": "Any objective rule that defines eligibility for a social transfer program will irrationally exclude some persons.... Whenever the people who administer the programs run into a case of a genuinely needy person who has been excluded under a current rule, they tend to redefine the rule or otherwise alter the program's administration to be more inclusive, which in turn brings more people who don't need the social transfer under its umbrella." This means that, even as people worry about how to pay for the existing program, there are calls to make the program more expensive.

Debates over what to do about Social Security invite intractable rhetoric. Consider a 2015 piece from the AARP, "Updating Social Security for the 21st Century: 12 Proposals You Should Know About," which includes brief pro and con statements from two experts, one from the conservative Heritage Foundation who favors controlling the growth of benefits and opposes raising Social Security taxes, the other from the nonpartisan (but apparently liberal) National Academy of Social Insurance who favors raising revenue and opposes cutting benefits. Here, we look at examples of these experts presenting arguments against various proposals (You've Earned a Say 2015). First, watch how the expert from the National Academy of Social Insurance dismisses various proposals to bring Social Security benefits under control:

- Raise the age at which full benefits are paid, in response to rising life expectancies (e.g., to seventy in 2069): "Raising the full retirement age is a benefit cut.... We can afford to improve and pay for Social Security without benefit cuts."

- Adopt a chained consumer-price index: "The current COLA [cost-of-living formula] doesn't keep up with the inflation that seniors face because they spend more than other Americans for out-of-pocket health care costs and those costs rise faster than inflation. The chained consumer price index would make matters worse by reducing the COLA."

- Adopt means-testing (i.e., "reduce benefits for higher-income recipients and ... even eliminate benefits altogether from the highest-income households"): "Means testing would change Social Security from an earned right to welfare.... Means testing would be a huge breach of faith with working Americans who earned their benefits by paying in over the years."

Now consider how the Heritage Foundation expert resists proposals to increase the program's revenue:

- Raise the cap on the amount of earnings subject to FICA above $118,500: "This proposal would increase taxes on some middle-class Americans without fully fixing Social Security's financial problems."

- Eliminate the payroll tax cap: "[This] would make all Americans worse off by hurting the economy. High-earning workers ... would face very high marginal tax rates, discouraging them from working more, hiring additional workers or expanding their businesses."

- Increase the Social Security tax rate: "[This] would increase every worker's taxes, regardless of income. On the employer side, the payroll tax increases would result in higher labor costs, which would discourage hiring and encourage employers to move overseas or automate more production processes."

And those are just the proposals to cover Social Security's currently budgeted costs. The same article also lists justifications for making the program more generous (and therefore more costly) that are endorsed by the liberal expert from the National Academy of Social Insurance:

- Raise benefits: "Most seniors rely on [Social Security] for most of their income. Yet benefits are modest—$1,230 a month, on average. We can afford to improve it."
- Covering newly hired employees of state and local governments not currently under the system: "Social Security works best for everyone when it covers everyone."

In sum, it is easy to present reasons to oppose proposals to fix Social Security, whether they involve raising FICA taxes or reducing benefits. Notice how the rhetoric of opposition invokes concern for "seniors," "middle-class Americans," "all Americans," and "every worker," while it warns against "benefit cuts" and "welfare." As the authors of one detailed review of the debate declare: "We caution you to be wary of the rhetoric around the debate on Social Security reform and the assertions about the motivations of people who suggest significant changes to the system" (Schieber and Shoven 1999: 10). Any change to Social Security taxes or benefits will inevitably have uneven effects—some people will benefit more than others, and some may even lose something. Most proposals to reform Social Security seek to avoid controversy by proposing gradual changes, so that tax increases and benefit reductions are scheduled in small, incremental changes that will occur years, even decades, in advance of the policy's implementation.

But this raises another issue—time. Let's say the best current forecasts are that Social Security will run out of money in twenty-five years, and that a small rise in the FICA tax, say 1 percent, will postpone the problem for three decades after that. But suppose Congress is reluctant to pass a tax increase this year. Next year, the price of fixing Social Security—the needed tax increase—will go up a bit, which means it will be even less popular, and so on, year after year. Delaying makes things worse.

Thus, predictions about Social Security running out of money are very different from those warnings about what the Maya calendar forecast. Even those who believed the Maya predictions could not agree about what was to come or why it would occur, and the vast majority of people simply did not believe that an ancient, carved-stone calendar offered authoritative predictions about the future. In contrast, forecasts about the future of Social Security are widely accepted. Notice that the debate over Social Security is hardly unique. If anything, funding Medicare—another very expensive, very popular program— poses even greater long-term problems. To be sure, most taxpayers and beneficiaries have imperfect understandings about how Social Security actually works, but those who understand the program can agree about what is going to happen. But that does not mean they can agree on what ought to be done. Critics have long noted that entitlements are difficult to reform. There are lots of different ways to address projected shortfalls in Social Security, and they all disadvantage some people more than others. This means it is always possible to organize opposition against any proposal, which has the effect of (a) making it easy to postpone acting (thereby making the problem slightly worse), and (b) encouraging compromise solutions (e.g., by both raising taxes and tightening benefits). But these compromises merely postpone the reckoning until the next cycle of calls to fix Social Security before it runs out of money in just a few decades.

WHY IS CLIMATE CHANGE CONTROVERSIAL?

Our third example involves warnings that global temperatures are rising, that human activities are causing that change, and that this process will have devastating consequences. Initially, this problem was termed *global warming;* more recently it has been rebranded *climate change.* These predictions have encountered a great deal of not just skepticism but also organized opposition.

The people who initially drew attention to climate change were scientists—experts usually thought to have very high standing in contemporary society. Pointing to trends in rising temperatures, they argued that these might be caused by human activity in the form of increased release of greenhouse gases that caused more heat to be trapped in the atmosphere. Climate scientists devised elaborate computer models to project what would happen in the future, and these models showed continuing temperature rises. This issue has come to be widely viewed as the most pressing environmental problem, having supplanted earlier concerns about overpopulation, pollution, and resource depletion. Obviously, these issues affect one another, but climate change has emerged as the marquee environmental issue—the subject of the most alarming claims.

Claims about climate change encounter more skepticism and opposition than warnings that Social Security is in trouble. Those who believe it is occurring express astonishment that scientists' assessments encounter resistance, and dismiss this reaction as "climate-change denial" (consider the parallel to "Holocaust denial")—a sort of willful ignorance. What explains the skepticism? Several factors seem to be at work.

To begin with, firsthand evidence of climate change is *ambiguous*. As individuals, we experience weather, rather than climate. Global warming became a celebrated social problem in the 1980s, when a series of unusually warm years culminated in the very hot year of 1988 (Ungar 1992, 1998). Some global warming advocates pointed to this unusual weather as evidence of climate change, which promoted public concern. However, when temperatures fell the following year, concern also dropped. A pattern emerged: climate-change advocates point to higher temperatures or other unusual weather, such as severe hurricanes, as evidence supporting warnings about global warming, but this leaves them vulnerable to their opponents using blizzards and cold winters to cast doubt on whether climate change is occurring.

Climate-change advocates are impatient with such weather challenges, arguing that climate processes are complex, but this *complexity* is a second factor that makes their job harder. Demonstrating the Social Security system's problems is child's play compared to explaining the elaborate computer models used to project future climate patterns. Assembling these models requires understanding all sorts of processes that are studied by scientists in a variety of disciplines—chemistry, physics, oceanography, atmospheric sciences, and so on—and then specifying how those processes interact. The resulting models seek to integrate knowledge held by all manner of specialists; the intricate workings of the entire models cannot be completely understood by the great majority of the people who contribute to them. Needless to say, most nonscientists are ill-equipped to fully understand these models. We find ourselves forced to concede that the scientists who specialize in climate processes consider these models the best available method for predicting future climate patterns, and that we must have faith in their expert judgments. Still, it is always possible to be skeptical about claims predicting the future.

Third, such skepticism is particularly easy when the threat seems *distant*. The scientists' computer models show gradual increases in temperature over a time period that, however brief it may seem to geologists, strikes most of us as long, as stretching into a future that we will not live to see. That is, the issue does not seem all that urgent, although climate-change advocates counter that we need to act now to ward off terrible consequences by, say, the end of this century.

And skepticism is fostered by a fourth factor: there is a well-funded, well-organized *opposition* to the campaign to draw attention to global warming (McCright and Dunlap 2000, 2003, 2011; Oreskes and Conway 2010). In particular, traditional fossil-fuel-energy producers—whose industries generate massive amounts of greenhouse gases—have waged a prolonged campaign to promote skepticism about global warming. In the United States, they have found political allies, particularly among Republican officeholders. This campaign has had some success: when pollsters first began conducting surveys on the issue, Americans of different political orientations were about equally likely to express concern about global warming; but in recent years, conservatives have expressed not only doubts about climate change but also less confidence in scientific authorities. This partly explains the effort to rename the issue: in response to the accumulated challenges to claims about "global warming," advocates adopted the new language of "climate change." This has had some effect. Polls find some Republicans rejecting the former while expressing concern about the latter.

The rhetoric of climate-change opponents shifted over time. Initially, the critics questioned the basic claim that global temperatures were rising; however, a growing body of evidence that temperatures were getting higher made it increasingly difficult to sustain this claim. A second line of reasoning was that global warming might be a natural process, that geological history shows that Earth has experienced cycles of global warming and cooling, and that today's rising temperatures might simply be evidence that another natural shift is under way. Again, a mounting body of evidence suggests that those higher temperatures are *anthropogenic*, that they are caused by human activity such as the production of greenhouse gases. There is a widespread consensus among scientists that the planet is warming, and that humans are responsible for at least a large share of the increase.

This does not mean every scientist agrees. Science itself is a human activity; scientists often debate one another, and today's consensus can turn out to be rejected tomorrow. The history of science includes instances when dominant interpretations shifted, when scientists who held formerly unpopular views were eventually vindicated. To say there is a broad consensus among scientists at one time does not necessarily mean that that interpretation will continue to be widely accepted.

In 1988, the United Nations helped organize the Intergovernmental Panel on Climate Change (IPCC) to synthesize scientific information and become the authoritative source for information about climate change. Every few years, the IPCC issues a long report summarizing the current state of the evidence. The documents are organized into sections dealing with specific scientific issues, with different scientists who specialize in those topics assigned the responsibility for writing particular sections. There are guidelines for writing these sections: basically, authors are responsible for summarizing the peer-reviewed articles published on their topic within a specific time period. In turn, their reports are evaluated and approved by the governments who participate in the review process. In effect, the IPCC has been an attempt to provide periodic, authoritative updates concerning what is known about climate change.

But the IPCC has also encountered skepticism. There have been critiques of various IPCC findings, most notably in a 2009 scandal that involved the release of email correspondence among members of a team of researchers at a British university who had been assigned to draft the section of the next report dealing with long-term climate change. This is a small but important section, because it makes the case that temperatures are higher and rising faster than at earlier times in history—which, after all, is the very foundation of the global-warming argument. This topic had attracted a set of skeptics who were continually emailing the researchers, asking for access to the raw evidence they had used in their own studies, so that they could better assess the scientists' published work. The researchers in turn emailed among themselves, and their correspondence was somehow released to the public. Their messages revealed some of the researchers saying a number of embarrassing things: that they were refusing to share their data with their critics; that they no longer had some of the data being requested; that they used what they termed a "trick"—a method of linking two sets of temperature data in such a way as to obscure some awkward findings; and that they had looked for ways to avoid including in their report some published results that challenged their views, while arranging to include some studies published after the deadline for the research they were supposed to consider in their review. In other words, they were making editorial choices that would let their section of the report seem more consistent with the larger global-warming thesis. The resulting scandal was quickly termed Climategate (Grundmann 2011). It was important because it seemed to confirm the skeptics' suspicion that the IPCC was not simply a dispassionate, scientific body, that some of its scientists were more concerned with presenting findings consistent with the global-warming thesis than with following their assigned roles to fairly summarize the available research.

Of course, scientists are human. They become personally invested in their work, and this can lead them to skew their findings. Much of the methodological apparatus of science, including double-blind experimental procedures, replication, and peer review, is intended to help keep the scientific process as honest as possible. The Climategate emails revealed individuals falling short of the scientific ideal, but these failings hardly prove that the larger climate-change thesis is false.

But there is another, more significant issue. Even if there is general agreement that temperatures are rising, and that human activity is causing at least some of the increase, it is not entirely clear what sorts of policies ought to be instituted to address this problem. Measuring the earth's rising temperature and accounting for the increases are scientific endeavors, much as building the first atomic weapons depended upon scientists' knowledge. But when it came to questions about whether to use those weapons, the decisions were made by political leaders, not scientists. In the same way, setting policies to deal with climate change is a political matter. Different policy choices are likely to have all sorts of effects: different industries will gain and lose jobs; different people may find their lives complicated, perhaps badly damaged; and so on.

It is important, then, to appreciate that skepticism about climate-change claims is not simply a matter of foolish people refusing to appreciate scientists' expertise. As we have seen, any prediction about the future is vulnerable to skepticism. Even when—as in the case of Social Security—the basis for the prediction is well understood, there may be bitter disagreements about the best way to address the problem. Agreeing that there's a problem does not mean there will be agreement about the best way to solve it.

And climate-change predictions are particularly challenging. Scientists' computer models are invariably imperfect: the accuracy of their predictions depends on assumptions imbedded in the models about the ways variables interact, and these may be flawed in various ways. For example, the models may fail to include relevant variables, or may incorrectly interpret how variables affect one another. Consider the much simpler challenges faced by meteorologists at the National Weather Service who seek to predict the weather for the next few days, usually for a particular local region (Daipha 2015; Fine 2007). Compared to forecasting global climate decades in advance, this is a simple problem, and yet it proves difficult; and the predictions—while better than they were a few decades age—still are often wrong. It is, then, clearly unreasonable to anticipate that climate-change predictions for the end of the century will be precisely accurate. Choosing the best policy responses to such uncertain, long-range predictions is not a straightforward matter.

THE LIMITS OF PREDICTIVE AUTHORITY

Although all three of our examples—the Maya calendar, Social Security, and climate change—involve warnings about the future, they have elicited very different societal reactions. As noted at the beginning of this chapter, all predictions face skepticism, but these examples reveal some differences in how predictions are evaluated.

Note that in all three cases, ordinary people are ill-equipped to evaluate the truth of the claims. We lack the qualifications, the knowledge, to confidently make assessments about the meanings of the symbols in the Maya calendar, about the financial stability of the Social Security system, and about likely shifts in the global climate. When we respond to such warnings, we cannot rely on our own personal experiences; our everyday lives do not offer an adequate basis for assessing the value of predictions about national, let alone global, crises. Nor do we have access to all—or even many—of the facts, or have the ability to properly weigh those facts and then arrive at some conclusion.

Rather than assessing the claims, we wind up assessing the people who make and who relay the claims. The sources for the Maya calendar prediction were largely individuals in the New Age social world. There have long been bookstores, magazines, publishers, and conventions that provide social support for those who believe in spiritualism, mysticism, numerology, astrology, flying saucers, and the like, and the Internet has offered additional ways for all sorts of folks—including those amenable to

New Age theses—to find and interact with one another. The Maya calendar prediction also received some attention via mainstream popular culture in the form of several television specials broadcast on the History and Discovery cable channels that featured interviews with various figures with New Age credentials—authors of books and the like.

However, the mainstream news media generally paid minimal attention to the Maya calendar prophecy, treating it as a fringe claim with little credibility. When reporters did cover the story, they often sought out people with establishment credentials—historians and archaeologists who specialized in studies of Maya civilization, including its various calendars. These experts did not credit the Maya with any unique understanding of the workings of the universe, and they denied that the calendar contained any apocalyptic message. Rather, they argued that it was just an arbitrary bit of recordkeeping, that the last day of the thirteenth *bak'tun* could be expected to precede the first day of the fourteenth *bak'tun*, much as this year's calendar ends on December 31, signaling the need for a new calendar covering next year beginning with January 1. Presumably, these scholars were perceived as having more cultural authority than those promoting New Age beliefs, and the mainstream news media's decision to ignore the issue led most people to assume that the 2012 predictions lacked substance.

In comparison, the sources for Social Security stories agree on the system's dynamics: that money flows in from FICA tax collections and back out in the form of Social Security checks. Anyone with a checking account understands such systems: when expenses continue to exceed income, there will be trouble. Moreover, there are generally accepted estimates of the number of people who will be eligible to collect Social Security and how much money they will be entitled to receive in succes-sive years, as well as how much money will be available to pay them. People can and do disagree about what might be done to fix the system—whether taxes should be raised, the benefit structure changed, or parts of the system privatized—but there is little dispute about what the future will hold if the current levels of taxes and benefits remain unchanged. Surveys suggest that a substantial proportion of Americans are aware of the debate about Social Security, and that they worry that upon retirement they will receive benefits less generous than those received by current recipients—perhaps no benefits at all. Yet even when the evidence for a prediction is relatively clear-cut, it remains difficult to organize a policy response.

All of this is in sharp contrast to the discourse regarding cli-mate change. At the one extreme, there are the climate change skeptics who claim to doubt the global warming thesis, who insist that every blizzard is proof that the world can't be getting warmer; at the other are those warning that rising sea levels and higher temperatures soon will make the planet no longer habit-able. Most of us are incapable of weighing the merits of climate-change predictions. For policy makers, as well as ordinary citi-zens, the issues are more complex than advocates insist. No wonder dealing with predictions is always challenging. But the three examples help us appreciate that thinking critically about future claims requires examining evidence and authority.

CHAPTER FOUR

Future Talk;
or, How Slippery Slopes
Shape Concern

To be convincing, predictions about the future must be presented in carefully chosen language. As chapter 3 noted, all predictions are vulnerable to skeptics asking how anyone can know what the future holds; the sorts of evidence used to support predictions make a difference in getting people to listen. This chapter focuses more narrowly on the words chosen to make predictions seem more persuasive. How does language shape our responses to predictions?

If we think about people who make their living forecasting the future, we realize that they often rely on *mystification* to package their predictions. Fortune-tellers, oracles, and the like often use bits of hocus-pocus (such as delivering their predictions in a darkened room, or staring into a crystal ball) and patter (such as offering assurances that they have some sort of gift, or second sight, that allows them to see beyond the present). Today, weather forecasters and those who peddle stock tips assure their audiences that they draw upon special expertise, and they may hedge their forecasts by speaking of probabilities rather than certainties (Daipha 2015; Fine 2007).

But not everyone can make their claims mystifying. Because advocates rely on convincing people that their predictions for the future are plausible, even accurate, they depend on framing those claims in rhetoric—future talk—that can persuade listeners. For instance, warning about the danger of a slippery slope is a common way of making a claim about the future seem more urgent. Although this chapter begins by examining slippery-slope claims, these are just one of the ways in which popular reasoning is used to frame the future that lies ahead. Other examples of such everyday language include claims about instances of some problem as being "just the tip of the iceberg," and claims that "we're only beginning to see" some impending change. In response to the criticism that the future is uncertain, all of these forms of future talk insist that common sense lets us have some confidence about imagining the way things are likely to develop. Forecasting the future of social problems is not restricted to experts with their projections and predictive models; it is something that ordinary people do in their everyday conversations, in particular when they imagine how things seem to be getting worse.

Although future talk is the larger subject of this chapter, we can better understand what's going on if we begin by looking closely at those slippery slopes.

ON SLIPPERY SLOPES

Back before Congress passed, and President Lyndon Johnson signed, the federal Medicare law in 1965, the question of whether there ought to be a federally funded insurance program covering senior citizens' medical expenses was being discussed, not just in Congress, but also by high-school debaters, including me. The topic was the national debate question in 1963–64, and our high school's debate team wound up reading many, many commentaries by people both for and against such a program. The opponents often warned that covering seniors' medical bills would be the first step toward socialized medicine; very often, they invoked a standard image and warned that a health-care program for seniors would be "a foot in the door" for socialized medicine. We encountered this image so often in our reading that it turned into an in-joke among our team's members. It became fun to work "That's just a foot in the door" into our conversations; we used the expression dismissively, in ways that suggested we were above such trite, fallacious arguments.

As it happened, my debate partner's father was a prominent official in the Kennedy and Johnson administrations. At one point, my partner spoke to his father about health-care policy and asked why the Democrats' proposals didn't offer more comprehensive coverage. He reported that his father had responded that the current proposal was "just a foot in the door," a precursor to more comprehensive programs.

That taught me that the foot in the door is a two-sided image: the expression can be used by opponents to warn about the danger that some minor policy change will pave the way for other, more significant changes; but it can also be used by advocates as a deliberate strategy—first we'll get people to accept this small thing, and then we can move on to eventually achieving bigger things. In both cases, it is a form of future talk, a prediction about what could lie ahead.

Note that there are other images that convey essentially the same idea. A foot in the door can also be described as a slippery slope, a camel's nose under the tent, a beachhead, the thin edge of the wedge, paving the way, opening the floodgates, giving an inch, crossing a line, standing at the edge of a precipice, entering a quagmire, opening Pandora's box, the domino effect, or a tiny acorn growing into a mighty oak (Stenvoll 2008; Volokh 2002–3). All of these threshold metaphors warn/promise that getting people to agree to some small thing can lead to far greater concessions in the future. I'm going to refer to these as slippery-slope claims, but the same facts apply to all of these metaphors.

Slippery-slope claims are a way of talking about the future. Instead of displaying evidence—such as actuaries' forecasts for shortfalls in Social Security funding or climate scientists' models predicting continuing increases in global temperatures—slippery-slope claims invoke a sort of popular logic. They say, in effect, that we all have personal experiences with how one thing follows another: we know that small concessions often precede and lead to bigger ones. Sexual relationships, for example, are sometimes described as developing in this way: one initially tries to "get to first base," then "second base," and so on. Whether you favor or oppose the bigger changes, slippery-slope imagery is predictive in that it encourages us to envision how today's small change might make it more likely that further changes are in the offing.

The Case of Same-Sex Marriage

Let's begin by examining some illustrations of the slippery-slope argument's two sides, as both warning and strategy. At the beginning of our new century, as one state after another legalized same-sex marriage, conservatives and Republican politicians advanced slippery-slope arguments warning about the dangers posed by allowing same-sex marriage to become legal. Senator Rick Santorum of Pennsylvania was outspoken: "In every society, the definition of marriage has not ever to my knowledge included homosexuality. That's not to pick on homosexuality. It's not, you know, man on child, man on dog, or whatever the case may be. It is one thing" (Associated Press 2003). U.S. Representative Louie Gohmert, too, was blunt: "When you say it's not a man and a woman anymore, then why not have three men and one woman or four women and one man? Or why not, you know, somebody has a love for an animal or—? There is no clear place to draw a line once you eliminate the traditional marriage" (Parnass 2013).

Similarly, Focus on the Family's James Dobson argued, "[The definition of marriage] becomes anything anybody wants it to be. So you could have polygamy. You could have incest. You could have marriage between a father and a daughter. You could have two widows, or two sisters or two brothers. Once you start that and put it in terms of rights, where somebody says, 'Why should I not have benefits if they get them?" then it's gone. You've undermined the entire legal foundation for the family" (*Hannity and Colmes* 2004).

Other commentators warned that there would be no way to block marriages to machines, ranging from U.S. Representative Steve King, who suggested that a man might now marry his lawnmower (Mathis-Lilley 2015), to one minister whose marginally less farfetched worry was about people marrying sexbots (robots designed to serve as sexual partners): "Without the Judeo-Christian worldview, the biblical template regarding human design and function was lost.... When biblically based traditional boundaries are ignored, we are not only left without general agreement regarding marriage, family and gender distinction, but we are also now left without boundaries related to the uniqueness of humanity as image-bearers of God" (Mattera 2015; cf. Marchant 2015).

In other words, these opponents argued, a society that accepted same-sex marriage would logically have to abandon objections to marriages between more than two people, close relatives, adults and children, people and animals, or even people and machines.

Such slippery-slope reasoning found its way into legal opinions. Consider Chief Justice John Roberts's dissent to the Supreme Court's 2015 decision legalizing same-sex marriage: "If not having the opportunity to marry 'serves to disrespect and subordinate' gay and lesbian couples, why wouldn't the same 'imposition of this disability' . . . serve to disrespect and subordinate people who find fulfillment in polyamorous relationships?" (Obergefell v. Hodges, 2015 U.S. LEXIS 4250).

These opponents of same-sex marriage did not always use the words *slippery slope,* but their argument was clear: moving beyond the traditional definition of marriage as an arrangement between one man and one woman by approving marriage of same-sex couples would place society on a slippery slope that could lead to accepting polygamy, incest, bestiality, and who knows what other sorts of relationships as legitimate bases for marriage.

These claims were not just denounced but also frequently ridiculed by those who supported same-sex marriage. Thus, Andrew Sullivan (1997) argued, "If you want to argue that a lifetime of loving, faithful commitment between two women is equivalent to incest or child abuse, then please argue it. It would make for fascinating reading. But spare us this bizarre point that no new line can be drawn in access to marriage—or else everything is up for grabs and, before we know where we are, men will be marrying their dogs. It is intellectually laughable." Late-night television comics had a field day with the topic, as when Jon Stewart mocked "bullshit slippery-slope arguments" (Dolan 2012).

However, it is worth noting that even as proponents of same-sex marriage denied that it placed society on a slippery slope leading to approving other forms of sexual relationships as a basis for marriage, the polyamorous rights movement (which remained carefully silent during the debate over same-sex marriage, so as not to lend credence to the opponents' arguments) did envision that acceptance of same-sex marriages would make it easier to gain eventual approval of polyamorous marriages. As one husband in a relationship with two women (he and his wife lived with their girlfriend) said, "If the majority is willing to take the big leap, it is hard to see how it can say no to the shorter one" (Polygamy.com 2015; see also Brekke 2015). Similarly, legal scholars began questioning whether laws regulating incest could be justified once same-sex marriage gained legal protection (Cahill 2005; Greenfield 2013), even as conservative commentators worried about signs that public support for incest might be growing (Brown 2012).*

In other words, while opponents made frequent use of slippery-slope warnings in what would turn out to be a losing campaign to block the legalization and acceptance of same-sex mar-

---

* The sociological literature has examined topics related to some of these processes. On the parallels and differences between the situations of same-sex and polyamorous relationships, see Sheff (2011) and Stacey and Meadow (2009). Similarly, the growing acceptance of homosexuality led to increased tolerance for other varieties of sexual behavior. Thus, the American Psychiatric Association's much-studied decision to stop classifying homosexuality as a mental illness also led to the demedicalization of "kink" (bondage, discipline, and so on; Lin 2017), while military leaders have campaigned to redefine post-traumatic stress as an injury, rather than a disorder (Smith and Whooley 2015).

riages, it was also the case that advocates of further extending the definition of marriage to include polyamorous relationships acknowledged that the success of the same-sex marriage campaign might well offer a foundation upon which they could build further challenges to traditional definitions of marriage.

Other Examples

While slippery-slope reasoning figured prominently in the recent debates over same-sex marriage, the same sort of reasoning appears in discussions of other contemporary social issues. Consider two: whether policies should be implemented to (a) restrict access to abortion, or (b) bring guns under tighter control. As I did in chapter 1, I have chosen two examples, because many people who are opposed to one are likely to favor the other. That is, in general, political conservatives are more likely than liberals to favor abortion restrictions, while political liberals are more likely than conservatives to favor gun control. Thus, these examples can help us appreciate that parallel slippery-slope arguments are used by people who favor different ideologies. Rhetorical devices know no ideology; they are cultural resources, available to all sorts of prospective users. People we agree with—as well as those with whom we disagree—may invoke slippery slopes.

ABORTION

Public opinion polls show that only a small minority of Americans (fewer than one-fifth) can be described as wholeheartedly pro-life—that is, as people who oppose abortion under all circumstances (Gallup Poll 2015; Smith and Son 2013). On the other hand, a larger proportion—roughly 30–40 percent, depending on the poll—adopt a firm pro-choice stance and favor making abortion available to any woman who wants one. The remainder—as much as half the population, in some polls—approve of legal abortion in some, but not all, circumstances. This pattern has been basically stable since regular polling on the issue began in the 1970s.

Because a substantial majority (more than 80 percent) favor legal abortion under at least some circumstances, pro-life forces have come to recognize that an outright ban on abortion is unlikely to gain support. However, it is also the case that only a minority of the public hold hardcore pro-choice views, while a majority express reservations about whether abortion should be legal in at least some cases. This has created a strategic opportunity for pro-life advocates, who have sought to restrict access to abortion services in a variety of ways, such as by setting regulatory restrictions on abortion clinics, establishing waiting periods, requiring an ultrasound examination before an abortion, requiring doctors to read scripts warning of the dangers of abortion, and the like.

Some of these measures may strike some people as modest and reasonable, but they are opposed by pro-choice advocates, who routinely invoke slippery-slope arguments stating that allowing whatever restriction is being proposed will set society on a path toward banning legal abortions.

- Elaine Werner, the executive director of the Connecticut chapter of the National Abortion and Reproductive Rights Action League (NARAL): "Any time I hear about giving rights to fetuses, I get concerned. That's a slippery slope toward eroding Roe v. Wade" (Apuzzo 2003).
- "Michelle Steinberg, an Arizona policy manager for Planned Parenthood, said women should never have to

make a case to get an abortion and called the bills
demeaning and bizarre. 'This could be a slippery slope in
terms of requiring women to disclose why they're
choosing abortion,' she said" (Muggeridge 2011).

· Jaime Miracle (2015), deputy director for NARAL
Pro-Choice Ohio, testifying against a bill limiting
abortion to the first twenty weeks of life: "It's a slippery
slope when lawmakers start specifying which procedures
are ok and which ones aren't."

Not all pro-choice slippery-slope arguments end with an
envisioned ban on abortion; they sometimes point to other troubling futures. Thus, Ilyse Hogue, president of NARAL Pro-
Choice America, responded to the Supreme Court's Hobby
Lobby decision (which said religious business owners need not
pay for health insurance that included coverage for contracep-
tion): "Allowing bosses this much control over the health-care
decisions of their employees is a slippery slope with no end.
Every American could potentially be affected by this far-reach-
ing and shocking decision that allows bosses to reach beyond the
boardroom and into their employees' bedrooms. The majority
claims that its ruling is limited, but that logic doesn't hold up.
Today it's birth control; tomorrow it could be any personal medical decision, from starting a family to getting life-saving vacci-
nations or blood transfusions" (Hogue 2014). At the same time, it
is possible to find those advocating additional abortion restrictions acknowledging that they see these changes as initial steps
toward an eventual abolition of abortion For instance, Americans United for Life president Charmaine Yoest commented on
the idea "that the pro-life movement needs to look for ways to
win smaller battles that build momentum and cut down on the

number of abortions that take place. 'We are working to push a boulder uphill, and you do that inch by inch and mile by mile,' she says. 'If there were a way to abolish abortion tomorrow, we would all be anxious to nail that down. But in a culture where there is as strong of support as there is for abortion, we have to keep focusing on the victories that are right in front of us'" (Alessi 2012: 27). Moreover, invoking slippery slopes in the abortion debate is by no means restricted to pro-choice advocates. Pro-life advocates also use slippery-slope arguments when arguing that legal abortion will lead to other, even more troubling social policies. Thus, conservative columnist Rebecca Hagelin (2012) warns,

> Decades ago, when Roe v. Wade was decided, conservatives and many religious folks predicted that the country had begun an inevitable slide towards a murderous future: a time when certain people—in addition to unprotected pre-born children—would be declared less valuable than others, their killing justified. Back then, liberal voices jeered at warnings of the slippery slope ahead. But those fears have become real. Medically sanctioned starvation and death-inducing dehydration are passed off as a "peaceful death" for the terminally ill or elderly. Our own President could not bring himself to vote, as an Illinois State Senator, to protect infants born alive after an abortion (they were simply left to die—which was what their mothers wanted, after all). And now, the advocates of death have stepped up the tempo. A new generation of ethicists has begun making the case in favor of so-called "after birth abortion." Like Princeton's Peter Singer, they believe that infants are not "persons" entitled to the right to life. Why? Because infants, while human, are not "self-aware." And these ethicists assert that human beings who lack self-awareness are not "persons" and, if they are not persons, then they have no independent moral status, no automatic right to life, and no claim to the protections of law.

Because the abortion debate involves opponents with incompatible objectives (eliminating all abortions versus making abortions widely available), it seems to be easy to construct slippery-slope arguments to the effect that any change inevitably will lead to additional, bigger changes.

GUN CONTROL

Slippery-slope arguments are also common among those opposing gun control measures:

- "Beware that while 'reasonable compromises' proffered by gun control proponents may sound disarmingly well-intentioned, many of these are certain to establish precedents for private gun ownership restrictions which are literally disarming" (Bell 2013).

- "Gun proponents, constitutionalists and those true to our country's values and traditions simply aren't interested in any further restrictions on America's second amendment, and they see smart gun technology as a slippery slope to further gun control" (Gommo 2015).

- "For more than three decades, the NRA has consistently argued that pretty much any new regulation of firearms would move the country a step closer to more draconian regulations, like gun registration and confiscation. The slippery slope argument has underscored most of the gun owner lobby's major messaging campaigns, and successfully helped rally a core group of Americans to oppose even the most incremental new measures, and become members of the organization" (Scherer 2013).

This stance has allowed gun-control advocates to dismiss slippery-slope arguments as unfounded. Thus, President Obama denied that his proposals would lead to a slippery slope: "Today, background checks are required at gun stores. If a father wants to teach his daughter how to hunt, he can walk into a gun store, get a background check, purchase his weapon safely and responsibly. This is not seen as an infringement on the Second Amendment. Contrary to the claims of what some gun rights proponents have suggested, this hasn't been the first step in some slippery slope to mass confiscation" (Obama 2016).

Similarly, a gun control advocate identifies two reasons why the slippery slopes are central to the opposition's campaigns:

> First, because it is so obviously difficult for the pro-gun forces to persuasively argue that many reasonable and popular measures—such as waiting periods, background checks, licensing and safety training, registration of gun sales, curbs on large-volume gun sales, and mandatory consumer-safety standards—are objectionable in their own right, it becomes essential to argue that these measures will ultimately lead to policies that have far less popular support and may be more difficult to justify.... Second, the NRA must sell the slippery-slope argument to convince gun owners and sportsmen that they have an important stake in the gun control fight. (Henigan 2016: 82–83)

However, gun-control advocates have on occasion articulated slippery slope strategies. Thus, in a 1976 *New Yorker* interview, one of the organizers of the National Council to Control Handguns explained, "We're going to have to take one step at a time, and the first step is necessarily—given the political realities—going to be very modest.... The first problem is to slow down the increasing number of handguns being produced and sold in this country.... And the final problem is to make possession of all handguns and all handgun ammunition ... totally illegal" (Harris 1976).

Moreover, gun critics routinely point to the much lower rates of gun homicides in other countries, which at least implies that these critics might favor the sorts of much more restrictive gun policies found in those nations.

In other words, there are rhetorical parallels between the ways slippery-slope arguments are used by proponents and opponents of tighter restrictions on both abortions and gun.

Are Slippery-Slope Arguments Fallacious?

Critics sometimes classify slippery-slope reasoning as a form of logical fallacy, an illegitimate form of argument. One philosopher acknowledges that "the textbooks have tended to treat the slippery slope argument as a fallacy, generally. Some textbooks portray it as a type of argument that is inherently fallacious, while others present it as a kind of argument that is, if not always a fallacy, one that may generally or most often be presumed to be fallacious" (Walton 1992: 15).

The reasoning behind such dismissals is that slippery-slope arguments need not be true—that is, making a small concession now need not inevitably lead to greater concessions in the future. No doubt this is correct. We can all point to small steps that did not lead to greater changes, at least in the short—and medium—run. To return to my high school debate topic, those critics who warned that providing government-funded health care for senior citizens would inevitably lead to socialized medicine were wrong. After Medicare was established, it would be forty-five years before the Affordable Care Act (a.k.a. "Obamacare") would be passed, and that program falls far short of the sort of national (i.e., "socialized") health-care systems found in western European countries. In other words, the predictions embedded in slippery-slope arguments are not necessarily correct.

But pointing to examples of slippery-slope reasoning that proved to be false is not the same as proving that such arguments are always fallacious. Our philosopher continues: "We need to rethink the concept of fallacy, redefining a fallacy as a basically reasonable type of argument which has been used in a bad or corrupted way in a given instance.... In other words, every good kind of argument, which can be used reasonably to further legitimate goals of dialogue, also has potential for misuse" (Walton 1992: 27).

The cases we've examined—same-sex marriage, abortion, and gun control—all show that both advocates who favor and those who oppose social policy changes recognize the relevance of slippery-slope reasoning. When opponents of some policy change worry that small concessions may lead to greater demands, they are warning that proponents of the change are likely adopting a slippery-slope strategy, that they will not settle for small changes and can be expected to push for further, greater changes. Moreover, this fear is not unreasonable, since we indeed can find advocates of change articulating slippery-slope strategies and advancing minor proposals as a means of pursuing a long-range goal. Thus, many of the pro-life state legislators who favor laws requiring physicians who perform abortions to have hospital privileges (a change that may make it more difficult for abortion providers to continue to operate, without making the procedure illegal) also acknowledge that they have a larger, long-range goal of overturning *Roe v. Wade* and ending legal abortion. Similarly, proposals to block gun purchases by individuals on terrorism watch-lists are unlikely to have much effect on gun violence, but the people doing the proposing often contrast levels of gun violence in the United States with those in countries that have much tighter systems of gun control, which implies that they are likely pursue further restrictive policies.

Part of the attraction of pursuing small, incremental changes is that they sound reasonable. Doesn't it make sense that abortion providers should be able to admit their patients to local hospitals if something goes seriously wrong (even if the chances of that happening are very low)? Why shouldn't we try to block people on terrorism watch-lists from buying guns (even if such measures are highly unlikely to prevent those people from obtaining firearms through some other means)? It is the opponents of such commonsense measures who seem unreasonable, whose railing about slippery slopes seems unhinged.

Gilbert (1996: 114) argues that a staircase is a better metaphor than a slippery slope: "Most situations are not at all like slippery slopes, but more like staircases: At each step you can stop and decide if you should go on by examining the next step down" (see also Henigan 2016). In other words, there is not an inevitable slide toward some extreme outcome. Consider the regulation of motor vehicles (discussed in chapter 1): laws requiring the licensing of cars, drivers, and so on are widely accepted; but they have not led to efforts to ban or confiscate cars.

At the same time, it is possible to point to examples of slippery slopes that seem to have shaped social policy. Medicare may not have led inevitably to socialized medicine, but the Social Security system has expanded over the decades to encompass a growing number of beneficiaries (Béland 2005; Schieber and Shoven 1999). Recall Charles Murray's "Law of Imperfect Selection" (discussed in chapter 3), which suggests that coverage for entitlement programs tends to involve a slippery slope. If slippery slopes are not inevitable, it is at least the case that some slopes turn out to be pretty slippery.

ON ICEBERG TIPS

The slippery slope is by no means the only form of future talk used in social-problems rhetoric. Other common images are also adopted in debates over social issues. Consider, for example, warnings that some visible examples are just "the tip of the iceberg." This is a standard way of suggesting that, just as the great bulk of an iceberg is hidden beneath the water's surface, the full extent of some social problem is not appreciated. Thus, it is common for advocates to point to some disturbing incident and assure their audiences that this case represents just the tip of the iceberg (see, for example, chapter 1's discussion of typifying examples in claims opposing legalizing marijuana and advocating gun control).

The notion that many instances of social problems may go unnoticed is familiar to sociologists. Criminologists speak of the *dark figure* of crime—the proportion of crimes that go unreported and uncounted when authorities are calculating crime rates (Best 2012). This insight also proves rhetorically valuable for advocates, who can argue that official statistics underreport the true extent of social problems, that there may be more, even many more, unrecorded cases. Thus we find the image of the iceberg tip used in various professional literatures to warn about unrecognized cases of child abuse (Bacon 2008), elder mistreatment (Rovi et al. 2009), child trafficking (Hynes 2015), gender transitions (Taylor et al. 2011), and other social issues. It also appears in public debates; for instance, icebergs seem to be common on our southern border, where advocates on both sides of the immigration debate insist that the known numbers of both reported deportation cases and child immigrants are just the tips of their respective icebergs (*FOX News Insider* 2014; Giovagnoli 2010).

In many tip-of-the-iceberg claims, the real issue is the size (and composition) of the iceberg. Commonly, the examples that advocates choose in order to typify social problems are calculated to disturb; they are especially troubling cases. Calling a troubling typifying example the tip of the iceberg implies, not simply that there are many more unseen cases, but also that those cases, too, will be troubling. The British sociologist Frank Furedi (cf. 1997, 2009, 2012, 2013a,b) has drawn attention to the expression's use in all sorts of claims: "That phrase evokes a terrible problem which we can only imagine but cannot accurately visualise. What we saw was merely the tiny tip of an unbounded peril of gigantic proportions" (2013b). A shocking incident in news reports is easily transformed into just one instance of a much larger problem. Thus, Furedi (2015) notes,

> Modern slavery has become an all-purpose portmanteau category into which every form of unpleasant and oppressive labour-related practice can be inserted. Cheap labour in a developing society, especially when it involves young people, is frequently classified as slavery.... The absence of facts frees advocates of the modern-slavery campaign to speculate at will. Just listen to [Jeff Nesbit, a former White House communications director]: "It could be more than at any time in human history. It might be less (though that's doubtful). What is true is that there are millions who are trapped, with virtually no recourse." Almost imperceptibly, the statement "it could be more" turns into the unassailable truth that there are "millions who are trapped."

This is a rhetorical flourish that can be applied to almost any social problem, a way of giving almost any remarkable story larger significance. No wonder that journalists so often report sightings of iceberg tips:

- "[A study] connecting porn and sexual aggression ... points to the tiniest tip of the iceberg when it comes to pornography's destructive influence on American society. Porn is literally polluting the minds and ripping up the souls of tens of millions of Americans. It is leading huge numbers of people into relational failure, family breakdown, heartbreak, addiction, misery, and disease" (*WorldNetDaily* 2016).
- "In the current craze to deploy conscience arguments to scuttle unpopular provisions of the Affordable Care Act, birth control is just the tip of the iceberg" (Lithwick 2013).
- "Law-enforcement issues, such as marijuana-intoxicated driving and the illegal movement of vast amounts of cannabis product into other states [in the aftermath of Colorado's referendum to legalize recreational marijuana], are the tip of the iceberg" (Haun 2015).

Claims about iceberg tips invoke the future in at least two ways. First, they predict that we will eventually discover that a problem's magnitude is much greater than we might imagine. When the news media report a terrible crime, advocates can declare that crime is just a visible instance of a vastly larger number of similar yet invisible crimes awaiting recognition, acknowledgment, and action. Second—as all students of the *Titanic*'s history know—it is not the visible tip of the iceberg but its larger hidden mass that threatens to do the real damage. Ignoring the problem's true extent can have serious consequences. Moreover, these warnings are difficult to refute: how can anyone prove that a hidden social problem is not real—and dangerous?

Just as the slippery slope can be a strategy to promote change—and not simply a figment of the imaginations of those who oppose change—some sightings of iceberg tips prove correct. For instance, a 1982 article in the *New York Times* quoted public health officials saying that the number of diagnoses of GRID (for gay-related immunodeficiency) "probably represent 'just the tip of the iceberg'" (Altman 1982); this prediction can hardly be faulted for exaggerating the impact of what would later be called HIV/AIDS.

Slippery slopes and icebergs (which have slippery slopes in real life) are familiar metaphors, images intended to help us envision the future. They are cultural resources that are readily available to be used by virtually anyone in the service of pretty much any cause. They invoke commonsense reasoning to make claims about future social problems seem more convincing.

ENVISIONING CHANGE ON THE NEAR HORIZON

There are other conversational touchstones, not necessarily full-fledged metaphors that evoke clear images like those of slippery slopes and icebergs, but at least conventional phrasings that play similar metaphorical roles in shaping claims about social problems in the future.*

"We're Beginning to See"

Consider the phrase "we're beginning to see" (often "we're just beginning to see"). It tends to be inserted in conversations about

---

* Lakoff and Johnson (2003) argue for the centrality of metaphors in all human thought.

some minor yet troubling phenomenon: for example, "We're beginning to see that some young people are X-ing." This expression takes its power not so much from the speaker's claim that some young people are doing X as from the implicit suggestion that this is just the beginning of what will be a larger trend. That is, while it may be true that very little X is happening today, listeners are invited to share the speaker's suspicion that X-ing will spread, that there will be far more X-ing in the future.

The expression is invoked to herald positive as well as negative trends:

- "'Football is resting on this foundation of parental and cultural and masculinity-issued support that could be pushed to the background once people start to realize that taking the chance of brain damage isn't worth proving that you're a particular kind of man,' [sports sociologist Jay] Coakley said. 'We're beginning to see the erosion of that support'" (Shpigel 2012).

- "Elizabeth Sweet, who studies gender-based toy marketing at the University of California at Davis, said toys today are more gender-specific than at any time in a century. But parents are becoming more vocal about the issue, she said, and that is putting pressure on companies to respond. 'We're beginning to see the shift in large part due to the parents and other activists saying, "Hey, we need something different out there," Sweet said'" (Halzack 2015).

- "We're beginning to see a narrowing of the achievement gap between white students and other students" (Kennedy 2008).

- "Simon Antrobus, who works for the drug and alcohol treatment charity Addaction, is hopeful that the proposals will increase public awareness. 'We're beginning to see people thinking, "I have to do something about this,"' he said" (Hui 2012).

In each case, there is the implication that today's small changes are harbingers of greater things to come.

"We're beginning to see" resembles slippery-slope arguments in that both suggest that the future will develop along a particular path, that what might seem to be today's small matters will lead to greater consequences tomorrow. However, while references to slippery slopes suggest a mechanism by which this might happen—today's small concessions will make it harder to block much larger ones in the future—"we're beginning to see" does not explain how or why the future will develop. Rather, it sees today's X-ing as a harbinger, as an early adoption of what seems likely to become a growing trend. The expression's effectiveness depends on an appeal to the listener's common sense (that is, if some people are doing this now, then surely more will follow).

Just as there many threshold metaphors equivalent to the slippery slope, there are other expressions that resemble "we're beginning to see." Consider *Body Count: Moral Poverty . . . and How to Win America's War against Crime and Drugs,* a 1996 book by former drug czar William J. Bennett and two other conservative public intellectuals (Bennett, DiIulio, and Walters 1996). This book forecast that the beginning of the twenty-first century would be marked by a dramatic rise in crimes by juvenile "superpredators." Notice the different bits of future talk used to make this claim seem convincing:

Like *the frog who will jump out of scalding water but will allow itself to be parboiled in water that is heated slowly enough,* much of the American public has become inured and desensitized to the horrors of violent crime. (p. 13, emphasis added here and below)

America is a *ticking crime bomb.* (p. 21)

As high as America's body count is today, *a rising tide* of youth crime and violence is about to lift it even higher. (p. 26)

America is now home to *thickening ranks* of juvenile "super-predators." (p. 27)

This prediction is notorious because it was really wrong: *Body Count* appeared early in what would be a decadeslong drop in violent crime rates. Its authors were not unaware of the trend; they just insisted it was irrelevant: "Recent downward trends in crime mask an alarming rise in teenage violence.... We may be experiencing the *lull before the coming crime storm*" (p. 13).

The superpredator forecast is hardly the only example of a mistaken prediction supported by glib future talk. Take the menace of crack babies—infants born to mothers who smoked crack during pregnancy—who were supposedly born with neurological damage that would have permanent effects. When this concern was attracting lots of attention, Ellen Goodman (1989) began one of her columns with the following: "The poster on the hospital wall doesn't waste any words. Over the picture of a baby it says: 'Some of the people who take cocaine during pregnancy never get over it.' This is more than a public-service warning to pregnant women. It's also the bottom line from the research done on cocaine babies. Most never get over it."

However, projections that there were nearly four hundred thousand crack babies who would require extensive services from schools and other social services proved wrong; mothers who were addicted were almost always very poor, and their children born in addiction turned out to have the same disadvantages that other very poor children had, rather than some constellation of additional, special problems.

At the time they are uttered, it is difficult to assess "we're just beginning to see" claims. The expression seems to hedge, to suggest that there are signs that some sort of change has begun, that these developments are expected to continue. "We're beginning to see"—like other claims about boiling frogs, rising tides, and the like—makes a qualified, tentative prediction, an educated guess about what the future holds.

Tipping Points

Another metaphor that serves a similar purpose is "a tipping point," made fashionable by Malcolm Gladwell's book of that name (2000). Gladwell was writing about the process of diffusion—how ideas and the activities or products associated with them spread through populations. He argued that diffusion begins slowly, and then *tips* and dramatically picks up speed. The book was a best seller, and the expression itself took on a new life (or, if you will, hit a tipping point of its own).

As a result, advocates of all stripes now incorporate references to tipping points in their rhetoric. What is particularly interesting about this development is the way they use it to predict the course of future events. It is one thing to look back on the speed with which some innovation spread, note that it began to accelerate at some point, and declare that moment was its tipping point. But it is different to look at some process and forecast that a tipping point seems to be near at hand. Consider some examples:

- A *BBC Magazine* story titled "A Tipping Point in the Fight against Slavery?" quotes an advocate: "We have not quite reached the tipping point, but it's much more difficult for countries and companies to get away with forced labour nowadays" (Hogenboom 2012).

- From a website calling for expanding military defense capabilities: "I fear we are very near a tipping point, from which it will be difficult if not impossible to recover" (Cooper 2016).

- Environmental advocates warn: "Human activities are pushing Earth toward a 'tipping point' that could cause sudden, irreversible changes in relatively stable conditions that have allowed civilization to flourish" (Morello 2012). Alternatively, things may be looking up: "The world is approaching a tipping point, with renewable energy taking over from the fossil fuel industry" (Topping 2016).

Clearly, insisting that there is a tipping point on the horizon has become a cliché. The term sounds precise, even technical—here is the point when things started to shift. But people usually invoke this metaphor to predict a future course of events; advocates say we seem to be approaching/near/close to a tipping point. Most the articles cited above have titles posed as questions; these are not so much confident declarations of what is about to happen as speculations that things might be about to change.

Tipping points resemble "we're beginning to see" in that both expressions claim that some change is going to happen. This may be expressed as a hope for the change or as a worry about the change, but in either case the rhetoric serves to make an imagined future seem likely, to suggest that the crystal ball is clear, not cloudy.

THE ORACLE SPEAKS

Invocations of slippery slopes, iceberg tips, "we're beginning to see," and tipping points are conventional ways of providing rhetorical support for claims about the future of social issues. Warning of a slippery slope is overtly futuristic; it is a prediction that surrendering on a minor point today will lead to much greater concessions tomorrow. Similarly, "we're beginning to see" projects the extension of some sort of current trend into the future. Even talking about the tip of the iceberg has temporal implications, in that it warns that the aspects of a troubling condition that we are noticing now obscure the much greater, more serious aspects that we may well later find ourselves confronting.

We have already noticed that future talk about social problems is tricky. People have an imperfect ability to predict what's going to happen. Forecasts often prove to be wrong. In retrospect, upbeat predictions often seem to have been overoptimistic—you still don't have a flying car in your garage and are unlikely to have one anytime soon. On the other hand, warnings about impending disasters often turn out to have been unduly pessimistic. Excessive pessimism can be found in warnings about the future from conservatives who constantly worry that cultural changes (e.g., racial integration, same-sex marriage, etc.) will lead to societal collapse, but also from liberals (e.g., in warnings that concealed-carry gun laws will lead to gunfights in the streets, welfare reform will lead to starving children, etc.). The future rarely keeps up with the optimists' enthusiasm or turns out to be quite so bleak as the pessimists fear.

Every culture makes available a stock of cultural resources—metaphors, expressions, idioms, fables, folk wisdom, collective memories, and so on—that can be invoked to support arguments of all sorts. Speakers can incorporate these elements in their reasoning, with the expectation that many of their listeners will be familiar with, and perhaps reassured and convinced by, them. Because they are part of a shared set of ideas about how the world works, they make claims seem more reasonable.

This chapter and its predecessor argue that claims about social problems often feature predictions about the future. These range from explicit forecasts (e.g., "Social Security will run out of money in X years"), to vaguer, often implicit metaphors about what may happen (e.g., "We seem to be approaching a tipping point"). Clearly, there are lots of ways to shore up claims about what the future will contain, and they deserve critical examination rather than a free pass.

PART THREE

Looking Backward and Beyond Sociology

Memories as Problems; or, How to Reconsider Confederate Flags and Other Symbols of the Past

WRITTEN WITH LAWRENCE T. NICHOLS

Typically, social-problems claims focus on the present. That is, advocates argue that some aspect of contemporary society is disturbing—that poverty, crime, or some other troubling condition needs to be addressed. Sometimes, as we have seen, their claims also project into the future by making predictions that things are going to get worse. But claims can also look backward, constructing the past as problematic. The past is never set in stone; it is always up for reconsideration and reconstruction, and there are competing versions of the past. What sociologists call collective memories are never permanent or unanimous.

Many analyses of claims about the past are intended to place the present in context, to demonstrate that today's problems are not new, that they have a history. For example, in the 1970s, the term *child abuse* inspired reflections on the histories of the behaviors now deemed abusive, and also on earlier campaigns to problematize those behaviors under earlier labels. Thus, historians found records of adults beating or having sexual contact with children, accounts that could be reinterpreted as evidence that child abuse had a long history (deMause 1974), while Pfohl (1977) traced the history of campaigns against child cruelty (such as the Society for the Prevention of Cruelty to Children, which sought to piggyback on the success of efforts against animal cruelty). Of course, these interpretations ignored the changes in the meanings of these activities; many of those historical adults took their behavior for granted and did not view it as problematic. There is nothing unusual about presenting evidence that what is now receiving the attention of claimsmakers was—or was not—considered troubling in earlier time periods. In some cases, analysts argue that there are cycles of concern, that a social condition may become the focus of attention, then recede from view, only to reemerge as a problem once again (cf. Jenkins 1998).

In still other cases, it is our current understanding of the past that becomes the focus of claims. Sociologists who study collective memory argue that the past is not stable, that it is reinterpreted over time. In some cases, this involves people arguing that some earlier construction of the past is itself problematic, that it needs to be revised or replaced. For example, over the last fifty years, critics have argued that the versions of American history long taught in schools and colleges focus too narrowly on the actions of elite white males, and that this is problematic because it excludes the stories of women, ethnic minorities, and the working and lower classes. Typically, this has been presented as a problem that can be solved through addition—by adding stories about a more diverse set of people to American history. But history classes take up finite hours; they cannot simply be expanded. If some topics are added or expanded, others will inevitably shrink or disappear. What should be remembered can be controversial, with advocates of new collective memories struggling against those seeking to defend older interpretations.

CONTROVERSIES OVER THE CONFEDERATE BATTLE FLAG

Consider the recent wave of campaigns challenging the use of symbols that memorialize aspects of the Confederacy and other controversial historical topics. The initial focus of the recent campaigns was the use of the Confederate battle flag (hereafter CBF), particularly by state governments in the Deep South. The CBF has a long and convoluted history (Coski 2005). It, of course, originated during the Civil War, when it was carried by some Southern military units. In the decades immediately following the war, it rarely flew, except at Southern war memorials and cemeteries. However, Mississippi adopted a new state flag in 1894 that included the CBF in its upper-left-hand corner and, around the same time, Florida (1900) and Alabama (1895) adopted state flags featuring Saint Andrew's crosses (the diagonal cross also found on the CBF) that might be interpreted as symbolic allusions to those states' Confederate histories. These changes coincided with the rise of both lynching and Jim Crow laws in the post-Reconstruction South. In the middle of the twentieth century, the popularity of the CBF surged again; in 1948, it became a symbol of the anti-integrationist Dixiecrat campaign in which Strom Thurmond ran for president. However, the CBF still was not a particularly visible symbol in the early 1950s, when it became the focus of a "flag fad" that was popular in the North as well as the South and was widely seen as innocuous: "Even a contributor to the NAACP's magazine *The Crisis* concluded 'that the waving of the Confederate battle flag is just a fad like carrying foxtails on cars.'" (Coski 2005: 112).

However, by the late 1950s, opposition to school desegregation and the civil rights movement led to clearly politicized displays of the CBF that signified resistance to federal authority and/or support for white supremacy. The Civil War centennial (celebrated during 1961–65) added to the confusion: the American flag and the CBF were often juxtaposed during those celebrations. Southerners were concerned with how their history would be presented during the centennial celebrations, and there were tensions. The commemoration of the hundredth anniversary of the firing on Fort Sumter in Charleston, South Carolina, involved a national assembly of state centennial commissions. New Jersey's delegation included a black member, whose participation in events would have violated South Carolina's segregation laws. When that state refused President Kennedy's request that it make an exception, he "called for the national assembly to be moved to the Charleston Naval Base, a federal installation where South Carolina's segregation laws would not apply" (Prince 2004: 39; Cook 2007).

All of these factors combined to lead to new uses of the CBF to symbolize—to varying degrees—pride in the South and its history, generalized rebelliousness or independence, resistance to federal interference in the states, opposition to the cause of civil rights, and support for white supremacy. In the Deep South, these meanings shaped new, official state policies. Georgia made the CBF part of its state flag in 1956, and South Carolina and Alabama launched formal policies of flying the CBF over their state capitol buildings in 1962 and 1963, respectively—all official policies intended to express resistance to federal authority's support for integration (Martinez 2008; Prince 2004; Webster and Leib 2002). At the same time, the CBF became a more visible icon in popular culture about the South. College sports at Southern campuses often invoked the CBF: for instance, the University of Mississippi had long used CBF symbolism— including opening the "world's largest Confederate flag" during halftime at home football games (Newman 2007). Similarly, stock car racing had its roots in the South, and the CBF was displayed freely at NASCAR races. The heroes of the popular television series *Dukes of Hazzard* (1979–84) had a CBF design on the roof of their car; various country and rock musicians incorporated the CBF in album covers and T-shirt designs; and so on.

The symbolism of the CBF was multifaceted. First, it stood as a symbol of the military struggle in which it was carried, as when imagery for the Civil War centennial routinely juxtaposed the stars and stripes with the CBF. (While there was a national flag for the Confederate States of America—sometimes called the stars and bars—it was not as widely recognized or often used as a mobilizing symbol.) Illustrations of Civil War battles often depicted troops fighting beneath the CBF, and of course the CBF often flew at Southern military cemeteries and war memorials.

A second set of meanings concerned regional identity. Romanticism about "the Lost Cause" ran through collective memories about the Civil War, and the CBF served as a symbol of this Southern heritage, but also of a more general independence and rebelliousness. From the early 1950s flag fad to the *Dukes of Hazzard* and Southern rockers, the CBF was successfully marketed to audiences outside the South as a symbol of Southern pride. In 1992, when the Gallup Poll first asked a national sample "Do you, yourself, see the Confederate flag more as a symbol of Southern pride, or more as a symbol of racism?" 69 percent of Americans chose the former (Jones 2015).

But of course, a third set of meanings emphasized the racial connotations of the CBF and its symbolic connection to slavery, states' rights, racism, and support for white supremacy. The CBF was used by whites protesting the civil rights movement: it was displayed at Ku Klux Klan demonstrations and by opponents of school integration and civil rights demonstrations. Majorities of blacks—both in the South and nationally—objected to the CBF (Cooper and Knotts 2006; Holmes and Cagle 2000; Jones 2015; Webster and Leib 2001, 2002). There was also evidence that women reacted less favorably to the CBF (Hutchings, Walton, and Benjamin 2010). In the South, women, organized religion, and upper-class white males had once played leading roles in celebrating the Lost Cause; but they increasingly sought to distance themselves from the CBF and the working-class white males who now were its principal defenders (Brown 2011).

This third set of racial meanings gradually came to overpower the other two. "After the war against Nazi Germany and the civil rights movement of the 1950s and 1960s, objections tended to focus more often on the Confederate commitment to racial bondage than secessionists' disloyalty to American democracy. The observation that 'you cannot separate slavery from the flag, bottom line' remained the single most common historical argument against state display of the flag in debates at the end of the [twentieth] century" (Brown 2011: 47). It provided a focal point for campaigns denouncing racism by arguing that the CBF was a symbol around which some racists rallied, that it was intended to intimidate and terrorize in much the same way as a burning cross or Klansmen's hoods and robes, and that the CBF was a form of hate speech. Originally, these claims were directed at state flags that incorporated CBF elements, and at state governments actually flying the CBF at various locations. This became a particularly compelling argument: that state governments should not endorse a symbol that many people understood as not just racist but as symbolizing rebellion and therefore as unpatriotic to the United States as a whole.

This campaign gained ground in the 1990s. Alabama, Georgia, Mississippi, and South Carolina—the four Deep South states that either flew the CBF or had state flags with designs that prominently featured the CBF—had populations that were at least one-quarter black, which meant that their legislatures contained members from districts where many voters opposed the CBF; in many cases, their major cities were now majority black. In addition, CBF opponents began using economic pressure. Some firms had already begun backing away from the CBF: years earlier, the Six Flags Over Texas amusement park's Confederacy section had stopped flying the CBF at the section's entrance and selling souvenirs featuring the CBF; the section was renamed the Old South in 1997 (Mosier 2015). In 1994, activists called for an economic boycott of South Carolina's tourism industry. This was a potentially serious threat: during a boycott of Arizona after its governor rescinded the state holiday honoring Martin Luther King Jr., "the local tourism and convention economies were severely affected" (Holmes and Cagle 2000: 293). And now there were calls for boycotts in other Deep South states. In response, various entities in Georgia began announcing that they would no longer fly the state flag featuring the CBF: "The Atlanta-Fulton County Recreation Authority … voted unanimously to stop flying the Georgia flag in the Atlanta-Fulton County Stadium, where the professional baseball and football teams played their games.... [S]ome school officials, judges, county officials, and others in the metro-Atlanta area ... removed the current flag from their facilities.... The Holiday Inn and Hyatt Regency hotels and McDonald's restaurants removed the flag" (Holmes and Cagle 2000: 295–96). Some state business leaders—and some legislators who may not have objected to the CBF on principle—worried that their states' CBF policies might have consequences: decisions about where to locate a factory or host athletic tournaments might hinge on negative perceptions of their states' racial climates derived from displays of the CBF, either by itself or as a prominent element in a state flag.

In the face of arguments that the CBF was offensive, the Deep South states began to back down. After a series of court cases, Alabama stopped flying the CBF above its state capitol dome in 1993; the flag was relocated to the Confederate memorial on the statehouse grounds (Webster and Leib 2002). In 2000, South Carolina followed suit (Prince 2004; Webster and Leib 2001). (After further controversy, both states would take the additional step of removing the CBF from their Confederate monuments and their capitol grounds in 2015.) In 2001, Georgia changed its state flag from the 1956 flag (on which the CBF took up most of the space) to a more innocuous design dominated by the state seal above a ribbon that featured small images of five flags from Georgia's history, including the 1956 design with a now tiny CBF element (McNinch-Su, Richardson, and Martinez 2000). Only two years later, that design was replaced by a new one that completely abandoned the CBF, although the newer flag featured elements from the stars and bars—the much less recognizable national flag of the Confederacy. Also in 2001, Mississippi held a statewide referendum in which voters were asked to choose between the current flag (featuring the CBF) and an alternative design; the current flag outpolled the alternative nearly two-to one, with the voting "primarily, but not exclusively, along racial lines" (Coski 2005: 266).

These changes acknowledged that the CBF was at best a controversial symbol. The anti-CBF campaign gained new impetus in early 2015, when a young white man shot and killed several people at a black church in Charleston, South Carolina. The news media publicized a photograph of him posing amid guns and CBF symbols—which seemed to establish the link between the CBF and racist violence. (A contributing factor was a recent series of police shootings of blacks in 2014 and early 2015 that had inspired the Black Lives Matter movement.) Events snowballed: in South Carolina, critics demanded removing the CBF from the statehouse grounds; the state government originally argued that it was required by law to fly the CBF; a young black woman climbed the statehouse flagpole and cut down the flag; and when CBF defenders argued that the flag was not a racist symbol, critics pointed to its adoption by racist groups in Germany that were not allowed to display swastikas. The Gallup Poll reported that, between 1992 and 2015, public support for the CBF had declined—from 69 to only 54 percent viewing it as a symbol of Southern pride; among Democrats and blacks, substantial majorities (58 and 69 percent, respectively, saw the CBF as a symbol of racism (Jones 2015). The South Carolina legislature hastily revoked the law requiring that the CBF be flown.

The key step in the anti-CBF campaign was equating its meaning to racism. If one of the CBF's meanings was racist, than none of its other meanings were relevant; in fact it was possible to doubt whether those other meanings were not disingenuous. And since racism was now publicly understood to be completely unacceptable, then the CBF as a symbol of racism should be eradicated.

This, of course, raised a First Amendment issue. Courts have long held that waving—or desecrating—a flag is a form of protected speech (Welch 2000). Any American has a right to, say, wear a T-shirt featuring a CBF. So protests have centered on the display of the CBF by institutions. In particular, there were challenges to practices that implied approval of the CBF by government agencies. Consider federally administered veterans' cemeteries. Union and Confederate dead were often buried in different locations, and many of the national cemeteries operated by the National Park Service were intended for the Union dead. Still, there are Confederate troops buried at some of these sites, and there is an NPS policy that

> allows the Confederate flag to be displayed in some national cemeteries on two days of the year. If a state observes a Confederate Memorial Day, NPS cemeteries in the state may permit a sponsoring group to decorate the graves of Confederate veterans with small Confederate flags. Additionally, according to the NPS reference manual (p. 33), such flags may also be displayed on the nationally observed Memorial Day, to accompany the U.S. flag on the graves of Confederate veterans. In both cases, a sponsoring group must provide and place the flags, and remove them as soon as possible after the end of the observance, all at no cost to the federal government. At no time may a Confederate flag be flown on an NPS cemetery flagpole. (Comay and Torreon 2015)

The Park Service also oversees the major Civil War battlefields. The CBF is not flown over these parks, although it may appear in educational displays (e.g., "A selection of Confederate flags used to represent regiments in 'Pickett's Charge' during the 100th anniversary of the Battle of Gettysburg" (Gettysburg

National Military Park 2016). In 2015, the NPS director requested park superintendents to work with vendors to remove CBF souvenirs from sale at park stores: "All sales items in parks are evaluated based on educational value and their connection to the park. Any stand-alone depictions of Confederate flags have no place in park stores" (Gettysburg National Military Park 2015). Around the same time, other merchants, including Walmart, Amazon, and eBay, announced they would no longer sell products displaying the CBF, even as Warner Bros. halted licensing of toy cars modeled after the *General Lee,* the car from *The Dukes of Hazzard* with a CBF design on its roof (Derschowitz 2015; Lee 2015). In short, the CBF had lost most of its mainstream validation; only the Mississippi state flag remained, and there were renewed calls to replace it.

Its critics did not deny the CBF's place in history. They often argued that the appropriate place to display the CBF—and discuss its varied meanings—was in museums. Similarly, sets of toy soldiers and other products that symbolized the Civil War by juxtaposing the U.S. flag and the CBF were considered acceptable. It was contemporary, stand-alone displays that were no longer approved.

BEYOND THE FLAG

The spreading campaign against the CBF in 2015 set off a new round of critiques of other Confederate symbols, particularly on college campuses, where critical analyses of racism are readily available. The College of William and Mary announced that on its elaborate ceremonial mace—featuring dozens of elements reflecting aspects of the college's history—a small seal featuring a CBF would be replaced by some new emblem (Anderson 2015).

The same announcement also said that a plaque that "lists students and faculty who fought for the Confederacy and includes an image of the battle flag" was being moved to the college library's special collections room (Anderson 2015). Other colleges reported acts of vandalism against statues of Confederate leaders on various Southern college campuses (Jaschik 2015). Some campuses, such as the Universities of Texas and Louisville, responded by removing or relocating such statues.

The arguments for removing statues and other Confederate monuments paralleled those regarding the CBF: they were often located on public land and built and maintained with public funds (several Southern states have Confederate memorials on their capitol grounds). The Southern Poverty Law Center (2016: 5) released a list of 1,503 "Confederate place names and other symbols in public spaces," including monuments and statues, but also public schools, cities, counties, and even ten U.S. military bases named for prominent Confederates. Not surprisingly, the vast majority of these are located in formerly Confederate states and, like the various uses of the CBF, many were established as political statements affirming opposition to federal authority or civil rights:

> Two distinct periods saw a significant rise in the dedication of monuments and other symbols. The first began around 1900, amid the period in which states were enacting Jim Crow laws to disenfranchise the newly freed African Americans and re-segregate society. This spike lasted well into the 1920s, a period that saw a dramatic resurgence of the Ku Klux Klan, which had been born in the immediate aftermath of the Civil War. The second spike began in the early 1950s and lasted through the 1960s, as the civil rights movement led to a backlash among segregationists. (Southern Poverty Law Center 2016: 9)

Some critics argued that monuments were different from the CBF. They not only memorialized historical events but also could be seen as historical artifacts in their own right. In addition, many are large, heavy installations that are not easy to move. Suggested solutions included modifying monuments by adding plaques that contain contextualizing information, or adding countervailing monuments to aspects of black history (e.g., a statue of the slave rebellion leader Denmark Vesey placed in a Charleston park). Parsing these issues proves tricky. Thus, two historians argue,

> Flags by their nature are symbols of governmental authority, while monuments do not always carry the same weight. When South Carolina and other southern states fly the Confederate battle flag on state grounds, they imply official state sanction of what the banner stood for in the 1860s—the preservation of slavery—and in the 1960s—the maintenance of racial segregation. To be fair, Confederate busts in capitol buildings and monuments on capitol grounds also carry the imprimatur of the state. As such, they might be good candidates for relocation to museums. But the vast majority of Confederate monuments stand on public land—parks, university campuses, battlefields—not directly associated with governmental authority.
>
> … Taking down Confederate flags, but allowing properly contextualized Confederate monuments to stand, strikes the right balance between promoting a complete picture of the past and respecting the needs of the present. (Kytle and Roberts 2015)

THE POLITICS OF CONFEDERATE MEMORIES

The Civil War occupies a unique place in Americans' collective memories. It is not just a dramatic moment in the nation's history but also one that is especially accessible. Most of the key battlefields have been preserved as national parks that attract millions of visitors each year. There is a particularly rich historical record: virtually all of the combatants were Americans, and they spoke and wrote in a language that remains accessible to us; the Civil War was one of the first wars to leave a photographic record; and improvements in printing technology and the expansion of literacy meant that there were both hundreds of newspaper and magazine illustrations produced during the war and uncounted letters and diaries by the war's participants. This provides plentiful source material for books about the war, and some of these continue to find their way onto best-seller lists. They range from novels (*Gone with the Wind; Cold Mountain*) to histories by authors such as Bruce Catton, Shelby Foote, and James McPherson. There are, of course, Civil War reenactors, but there are vastly more Civil War buffs and people who have at least some interest in—and considerable knowledge about—the conflict.

This intense interest in the Civil War began as soon as the war ended. Pride and a determination never to forget led to countless monuments and memorials. In Washington, D.C., for instance, the National Register of Historic Places lists eighteen monuments commemorating the Union's efforts—fourteen celebrating particular generals or admirals. There are hundreds, probably thousands, of statues and other monuments in other Northern towns and cities. Many of these have lost much of their original meaning as collective memories have faded. Who now recalls that Washington's Dupont Circle has at its center a monument to Samuel Francis Du Pont, the admiral who supervised the Union's naval blockade of Confederate ports? Who outside the South remembers that Memorial Day was established as a holiday to remember those who fought for the North?

In short, sites of remembrance were extremely widespread—in the North, as well as the South. Harvard began planning for what would become Memorial Hall shortly after the conflict ended; the finished building included a transept featuring tablets with the names of the Harvard men who died fighting for the Union. Yale's Memorial was not established until 1915, when "enough time had gone by to permit the broader view"; it features the names of Yale men who fought on both sides in the war (Connecticut Historical Society 2016). Similarly, many states, cities, and towns established memorials to their dead.

These monuments had complicated meanings. On one level, they originally represented mourning, a way to honor the memories of those who had been lost (Martinez and Harris 2000; Kinney 1998). But they also typically revealed a considerable parochialism: Northern monuments celebrated those who fought for the Union, just as Southern monuments celebrated Confederates. When the federal government established permanent cemeteries to hold the bodies of fallen soldiers, these were intended only for Northern troops; thus, the Gettysburg Address was given at the dedication ceremony for a cemetery for Union dead (Neff 2005). It is no wonder that Southerners established their own cemeteries (without financial support from the federal government). Memorial Day did not originate as a way to unify the nation in the aftermath of the war's tragic costs, but as a way for citizens in Northern states to commemorate their dead. In response, a number of Southern states established—and some continue to celebrate—a Confederate Memorial Day.

A third level of meaning involved recalcitrance—Southern reluctance to abandon the Lost Cause, and resistance against federal authority and racial integration. This became increasingly evident as the nineteenth century wound to a close. This was when Jim Crow was spreading, and Alabama, Florida, and Mississippi altered their state flags in ways that alluded to the CBF. It was also when the focus of Richmond's Confederate Memorial Day ceremonies shifted: "Beginning in the mid-1880s, but gaining momentum in the 1890s and beyond, speakers tried to position the South on a higher moral and ethical ground than that held by the North by resorting to the language of racial and moral purity" (Kinney 1998: 264). And, as the Southern Poverty Law Center (2016) notes, this was when the number of Confederate memorials grew dramatically.

These diverse meanings explain some of the appeal of memorializing the Confederacy. On the surface, honoring one's dead always can be presented as a solemn, proper activity, just as taking pride in one's culture and heritage can be seen as legitimate. Yet these activities also can be ways of displaying resistance, even while insisting that their symbolism is appropriate and innocuous. Thus, Southerners could argue that the Civil War was fought over states' rights, not slavery, and that the CBF symbolized the romanticism of the Lost Cause, the valor of the troops who carried it, and the pride of their descendants, and so on. However, these defenses were becoming less effective as claims equating the CBF with racism gained broader acceptance, and as various government agencies and private firms backed away from its display.

COLLEGES, SLAVERY, AND MEMORY

The renewed controversy in 2015 about flying the CBF on the South Carolina statehouse grounds attracted extensive national attention, particularly on college campuses. Reports that statues of Confederate leaders had been defaced on Southern campuses led to debates about Confederate symbols at Northern institutions. Of course, there were relatively few statues of Confederate leaders at these sites, although at a panel discussion on these issues, the history department chair at the U.S. Military Academy at West Point noted, "While West Point rejected as traitors all Confederate veterans in the aftermath of the Civil War, ... the university in the 20th century began to honor some Confederate officers. Now it's rethinking some of those ties, ... based on the idea that Lee, military leader of the Confederacy, alone 'killed more U.S. Army soldiers than Hitler'" (Flaherty 2016).*

While the Confederacy had once been rejected as treasonous, the more common critique had become that its principal purpose was to preserve slavery, which was an ultimate expression of racism. And Northern campuses could be linked to slavery. For example, one of Yale's residential colleges was named for John C. Calhoun, a Yale graduate who went on to become a prominent antebellum statesman most often remembered for championing slavery and states' rights, while Georgetown University had financed its early operations by selling slaves and had named buildings for two school presidents who had managed those sales. After recent debates on both campuses, Yale choose to retain Calhoun's name as a way of confronting, rather than hiding the legacy of slavery, while Georgetown renamed its buildings and

---

* Finding appropriate ways to remember the Civil War has been a challenge. Initially, the dominant view seems to have been that the North should claim the privileges of victors and celebrate the South's defeat (e.g., by filling the nation's capitol with monuments to Northern generals). Later, there was an effort to reconcile, to view the war as a national tragedy and celebrate the virtues of the Americans who fought on both sides (by having a national centennial celebration or by naming some military bases in the South after Southern generals). More recently, the argument that slavery should always be at the center of collective memories of the war has been gaining traction.

considered creating a memorial to the slaves who were sold and their descendants (Jaschik 2016b; Swarns 2016).

The effort to expose and expunge the legacy of slavery went further—to campaigns against potentially offensive words. At Yale, the heads of residential colleges had long been called masters, a practice that had its roots in the Oxford and Cambridge college systems. Similarly, Cornell's university gardens were called the Cornell Plantations—*plantation* is another old word, one that originally meant "area under cultivation." Both terms had usages that predated slavery, and both had been adopted by the colleges without any reference to slavery; but critics argued that they were now commonly understood as terms used in the slave system. Yale announced that its masters would now be called "heads," while Cornell was considering alternative names for its cultivated area, such as the Botanical Gardens (Jaschik 2016b and Wexler 2016). Colleges were choosing to avoid controversies raised by words that evoked slavery.

A trickier case involved Princeton's relationship to Woodrow Wilson. Wilson had been not just a Princeton graduate but also a president of the university who had done much to enhance the institution's rise to national prominence. He had gone on to be New Jersey's governor, and then president of the United States during World War I, the moment when the nation became established as a world power. He had been the principal advocate of the League of Nations. During the rest of the twentieth century, Wilson had been an important figure in the Democratic pantheon, an advocate of domestic reform and internationalism. However, in 2013, he had been the subject of a well-received biography (Berg 2013) that, while it acknowledged Wilson's many accomplishments, also emphasized that he was a white Southerner who held racist views and who, as president, sought to resegregate the federal bureaucracy.

Princeton had long made much of its connection to Wilson with, for example, its Woodrow Wilson School of Public and International Affairs and its Wilson residential college. Activists called for removing the name of this racist, but the university announced it would retain it while adding contextualizing information (Baer 2016; Jaschik 2016a). The University of Texas had already moved statues of Wilson and Jefferson Davis to less prominent locations on its campus; there were criticisms of a statue of Thomas Jefferson (a former slaveholder who many believe to have fathered children with one of his slaves) at the University of Missouri; and so on.

INTERPRETING THESE ISSUES

Sociologists refer to the ways groups of people recall their pasts as collective memory. Research on collective memory examines how the complexity of the past is reworked into coherent narratives; often this involves celebrating the contributions of heroic figures, such as Washington and Lincoln (Schwartz 1987, 2000, 2008). These stories evolve over time, changing to reflect the shifting needs of the societies producing the recollections. Thus, Columbus has played very different roles in the stories told by various groups at different times: by patriots in the first years of the new republic; later by Catholics and, particularly, Italian-Americans seeking to claim their own piece of the American story; and more recently by Native American activists demanding acknowledgment of their victimization. So, a figure once widely considered to be heroic is now viewed with ambivalence, even redefined as a villain (Kubal 2008; Schuman, Schwartz, and D'Arcy 2005).

Shifts in collective memory are particularly common in the case of contentious topics, such as the American Civil War. Consider the case of John Brown, who in the years leading up to the war led violent antislavery efforts in Kansas and later at Harpers Ferry, Virginia. Brown may have been lionized as a heroic figure in the North, but he was viewed as a domestic terrorist in the South (Fine 2001). The facts support both views: Brown was a committed abolitionist who encouraged murders. He has largely faded from Americans' collective memory; there is a monument, but it is in out-of-the-way Osawatomie, Kansas; and the Harpers Ferry National Historical Park is overshadowed by the larger battlefield commemorations in the surrounding region.

Historians are leery of refusing to acknowledge complexity. They generally reject the simplistic notion that Columbus—or John Brown, Woodrow Wilson, or Abraham Lincoln—should be categorized as either hero or villain, good or bad. In *Historians' Fallacies,* David Hackett Fischer (1970: 136; cf. Bartow 2015) describes the *fallacy of presentism:* "In the name of modernity and relevance and utility, [presentism] sacrifices precisely that kind of knowledge which historians can most usefully provide: knowledge useful in the establishment of present trends and future tendencies." That is, historical presentism interprets the past from the perspective of the present, so if contemporary Americans view racism as a terrible evil, then the racist views of historical figures such as Wilson become a reason for viewing them as villains, and their statues should be removed or destroyed.

The alternative to presentism is to attempt to understand the past. What did those historical figures think and do, and why did they think and behave as they did? And at a second level, what explains the thought and actions of the people who later established memorials and monuments to those historical figures? This is why historians often favor adding interpretive plaques to monuments that can address the memorial as well as the subject, so as to locate the commemoration in its larger context—to acknowledge, say, how Woodrow Wilson's leadership in international affairs long overshadowed his efforts to resegregate the federal workforce.

All monuments are statements about, not just what the people who build them think is important to recall, but also about which recollections deserve to endure. Often there are controversies. Think of the debates over the designs for the Vietnam Veterans Memorial or the National September 11 Memorial and Museum (Wagner-Pacifici and Schwartz 1991; Simko 2015). Critics with varying points of view parse the meanings of a monument's different aspects—by appraising the statue's stance or expression, how the figure's hands are posed, and so on—in deciding whether to praise or condemn its message. Or consider how new presidents often rearrange the portraits of their predecessors in the White House corridors, to make different individuals more or less visible, so as to celebrate the accomplishments of some and downplay others'.

But monuments are built to endure, and the sentiments that those who built them thought worthy of expression may not resonate with the generations that follow. There is nothing new about these issues. Studies of collective memory often trace the shifts in how historical figures and events are recalled and interpreted. However, the rhetoric used to address these issues has shifted.

Decisions to memorialize individuals or events are often couched in a rhetoric of values: this memorial honors those whose actions demonstrated a commitment to what the group holds dear—patriotism, bravery, or whatever. Thus, those who defend the CBF argue that it stands for pride in Southern traditions, for respect for the men who fought for the Confederacy, or for independence, even as those who oppose its use insist that it must primarily be understood a symbol of racism. Such debates revolve around different people's interpretations of the meaning of some symbol, which is why these debates are difficult to resolve.

If there is anything different about the post-2015 claims about the CBF, Confederate statues, and other memorials to individuals who held racist views, it is the way they incorporate a new focus—constructions of psychological harm. These claims emphasize the psychological vulnerability of those who might find these memorials disturbing, and the harm that the memorials might induce, particularly among minority students who might be made to feel unwelcome at colleges that display them. Thus, interviews quoted students at Princeton:

> [Wilson's presence] "feels like a haunting, like there are people the university still holds to the God-like standard who really did not want me here, did not want me walking these halls." ...
>
> [Although people make the case that,] "'Yes, Wilson did some racist things, *but*... [,]' [t]here needs to be a message sent that there is no 'but' when there's that level of hatred toward people who are now members of the Princeton community." (Baer 2016)

Some critics argue that such claims about psychological harm can be placed in a broader context. Furedi (2016: 36) notes the growing attention paid to the idea of vulnerability: "Although society still upholds the ideals of self-determination and autonomy, the values associated with them are increasingly overridden by a more dominant message that stresses the quality of human weakness.... As a cultural metaphor, vulnerability is used to highlight the claim that people and their communities lack the emotional and psychological resources necessary to deal with change, make choices, and possess the emotional resources to deal with adversity."

Some critics linked such claims to a new variant of political correctness in higher education:

> The current movement is largely about emotional well-being. More than the last, it presumes an extraordinary fragility of the collegiate psyche, and therefore elevates the goal of protecting students from psychological harm. The ultimate aim, it seems, is to turn campuses into "safe spaces" where young adults are shielded from words and ideas that make some uncomfortable. And more than the last, this movement seeks to punish anyone who interferes with that aim, even accidentally. You might call this impulse vindictive protectiveness. It is creating a culture in which everyone must think twice before speaking up, lest they face charges of insensitivity, aggression, or worse. (Lukianoff and Haidt 2015)

However, other commentators dismiss the influence of political correctness as overblown (Hellerstein and Legum 2016).

Although, these analysts argue that calls to make campuses safer for vulnerable students depend upon putative inner, psychological processes, it is also possible to study social interactions—or the avoidance of interaction—around these contentious issues. For example, Holyfield, Moltz, and Bradley (2009) explore how white students at a Southern university campus defend the CBF while denying that it should be seen as a symbol of racism.

While names of buildings and figures on statues need not intrude on everyday life, some other targets of protest may. Thus, Yale's president, Peter Salovey, explained why Yale replaced "master" as a title for the heads of those colleges even though it retained the Calhoun name for one of its residential colleges: "I think it is very hard for students to call their residential college head 'master.' It is cringe-worthy for administrative staff, custodians, and dining hall workers to call the head of the college where they work 'master' in this day and age. The masters themselves had become uncomfortable with the title and wanted it changed" (Cole 2016: 45). That is, expecting a college's students and staff (many of whom might well be black) to address the college head as "Master Smith" created an interactional script many participants might find antiquated, uncomfortable—even offensive. Moreover, such titles are relatively easy to change (think of academia's earlier transition from *department chairman* to *department chair*). Less easily resolved are challenges to memorials and other symbols that have significant sentimental meaning for their defenders.

LESSONS FOR THE SOCIOLOGY OF SOCIAL PROBLEMS

Obviously, the past is socially constructed through both what we forget and what we choose to remember. Some troubled parts of the world, such as Ireland, the Middle East, and the Balkans, seem plagued by competing collective memories of centuries-old conflicts, whereas some totalitarian regimes make deliberate efforts to alter the historical record, to expunge awkward memories (King 1997). In contrast, the United States seems to benefit from a sort of collective amnesia, made possible by a relative openness to assimilating different groups, a readiness to gloss over the unpleasantness of the past, and the relative sizes of the populations supporting competing memories. Public schools and popular culture Americanize the young. To the degree that new ethnic groups were assimilated into the dominant culture and considered part of the American story (celebrated as the "melting pot"), the proportion of the population that aligned with the shared collective memory grew. Thus, the descendants of the once-despised Irish began to be considered Irish Americans and later just Americans—a process that was repeated for many other ethnicities. This process was not easy or perfect. There was discrimination to be overcome, but over time the barriers encountered by various ethnic and religious minorities declined. The transition was never complete: different groups retained some of the old foodways and such, and some people remained more conscious of their ethnic group's past than others did, but it was possible to think of a larger portion of Americans as sharing a common collective, national memory.

In recent decades, these tendencies have been challenged by campaigns to acknowledge and celebrate portions of history that had been minimized. Thus, the calendar now features Black History Month and Women's History Month, to say nothing of Asian Pacific American Heritage Month, Jewish American Heritage Month, Hispanic-Latino Heritage Month, Italian American Heritage Month, and American Indian Heritage Month. Similarly, there are efforts to ensure that schoolchildren encounter diverse sorts of Americans, not just in classes on history and literature but also in the characters mentioned in arithmetic word problems, and so on. Education has become more inclusive in its celebration of diversity, usually in ways that suggest how all sorts of people have contributed to the American story.

From this point of view, the Civil War poses particularly difficult challenges to Americans' collective memories. A substantial minority of Americans lived in the Confederacy, and the South continues to be a major geographic region. There have always been more Southerners than members of any ethnic minority in the United States. The war's end hardly halted anger and resentment on either side—as evidenced by those separate monuments and separate cemeteries, to say nothing of the military occupation of the former Confederate states during Reconstruction. These conditions fostered the emergence of a distinctive regional collective memory that favored romanticized Lost Cause rhetoric, which allowed Southerners to celebrate their soldiers' gallantry while downplaying slavery's role in causing the war.

While slavery's end became a settled issue, the emergence of Jim Crow allowed the South to enforce a regimen of white supremacy beyond the end of the Second World War. The South gradually became less insular, less culturally distinct, even as the black civil rights movement gave voice to those who had been largely silenced. The federal government became more active in passing and enforcing civil rights laws. National public opinion polls showed that Americans were less willing to express racist attitudes. The bitterness over the Civil War receded, at least in Northern memories; Civil War battlefields became major tourist attractions, with a focus on the military story giving evenhanded attention to the generals, troops, and tactics on both sides. Geographic mobility—some Southerners leaving for other regions, even as more non-Southerners moved into the South—also meant that a growing proportion of Southerners lacked strong ancestral ties to the Confederacy.

All of this created opportunities for a South that could forgo clinging to its rebellious past. Insistence on celebrating the Confederate cause became likely to offend a growing number of categories of people, including not just blacks but also women and those with more education and more income who had a greater stake in the nation as opposed to the region, in the future rather than the past. Thus, the CBF became increasingly associated with "rednecks," with rural, pickup-driving, working-class males—a sector of the population that was shrinking and losing political power.

The 2015 controversy over the CBF on South Carolina's statehouse grounds was part of a decadeslong process that minimized the Confederacy's legacy. Claims that viewed the Lost Cause as noble had less and less resonance, with fewer and fewer people, particularly as people became more skeptical about claims that the Civil War's principal cause was not slavery. Thus, state governments gradually backed away from the CBF, prodded by officials in now majority-black cities who were rejecting CBF symbolism, as well as by business leaders who wanted to avoid offending customers and investors.

These events can help us think about the conditions under which collective memories are likely to be problematized. The first of these is that *size* matters. Collective memories are commonly tied to particular groups within a society—ethnicities, religions, or—in the case of the South—regions. The larger a group is, the more people there are who may favor some divergent collective memory. As we have already noted, the South accounted for a larger population than, for example, various ethnic groups.

A second factor is *isolation,* which often takes the form of geographic concentration. To the degree that a group's membership has many contacts with one another, and relatively few contacts with outsiders, it will be easier for them to create and maintain distinctive collective memories. Having people concentrated in a particular locale, whether it is an ethnic enclave in a city or a larger region like the South, makes it easier to defend alternative visions of the past.

Third, there is the matter of *resources*. Collective-memory maintenance can consume time, effort, and money. The more resources a group has, the easier it will be to promote their particular version of the past. While it took time to recover from the shock of losing the Civil War, by the 1890s the memory of the Lost Cause was being actively promoted—in the adoption of state flags that made symbolic allusions to the Confederacy; in the construction of monuments (often at public expense) and the celebration of holidays such as Confederate Veterans Day; and in histories written by Southerners, and taught primarily at Southern universities, that insisted that the war was over states' rights rather than slavery; and so on. The control over public schools and colleges, as well as over state and local governments, made it possible to promote collective memories about the Lost Cause. Of course, the reestablishment of white control over a disenfranchised black population denied voice to the group most likely to dispute these collective memories.

The gradual decline of the CBF can be understood as reflecting changes in these factors: the South remained a large region, but it grew less isolated during the twentieth century, thanks to greater interregional migration and the increasing importance of a national media and popular culture. This allows us to recognize the importance of a fourth condition: a supportive *cultural context*. Schwartz (2008: 17) argues that ours is a "post-heroic era:

> As the lives of the great are cynically scrutinized for cruelty, treachery, prejudice, and egotism, the growth of racial, religious, and ethnic justice, real equality of opportunity, compassion, and the recognition of minority achievement and dignity expands.... The multicultural ideal, as understood in the late twentieth century, encourages racial and ethnic groups to cultivate their historical uniqueness and at the same time recognize one another's equal

worth. Because historical wrongdoings violate these principles, multicultural elites replace monuments to heroes with monuments to victims; they replace symbols of strength and dignity with symbols of malevolence. Monuments of regret, including Civil War prison camp memorials, Japanese internment camp sites, exhibits, and memorials, Indian massacre sites, civil rights memorials, slavery museums, and lynching exhibits abound as historical texts document America's crimes against its own pluralistic ideal.

These shifts in the larger culture helped foster the prominence of a counter-Confederacy narrative within the South, where the CBF and Confederate monuments—long presented by white elites as symbols of Lost Cause heroism—could be challenged, particularly in urban areas where blacks controlled public institutions.

In other words, we can envision history as a sort of competition among collective memories. This should not be understood as a free-for-all. There are historians—people whose profession involves understanding and interpreting the past, and who are often granted authority as experts. But historians disagree about matters of interpretation—they may argue about the strength of evidence, and so on. History is inevitably selective: no American history class can possibly cover everything. It is always possible to debate what should or should not receive attention.

In much the same way, popular constructions of the past contend for ratification. And this competition among collective memories is likely to be shaped by the four factors we've identified: the relative sizes of populations attached to different collective memories; their degree of concentration; their resources; and the degree to which the larger culture is receptive to their claims.

What makes the recent debate striking is the way that statues, names of buildings, and other memorials, which of course were designed to be enduring reminders of collective memories, have become controversial. On the one hand, debates over the meaning of the past can be seen as evidence of a culture's resilience and strength: "In liberal societies, multiple versions of the past can safely coexist. An all-powerful, monolithic version of the past will not triumph in a pluralistic society where conflicting views have a good chance of emerging, finding an audience, and surviving. This is not to say that dominant views do not exist, simply that—again, in a liberal society—they are never invulnerable" (Schudson 1992: 208).

There was never a point when no one found the CBF offensive, and there may never be a time when everyone agrees that it is a social problem. But the recent developments seem dramatic precisely because—at least so far as the CBF is concerned—the dominant view has shifted, from that of people who favor the flag to that of its opponents.

We readily agree that the future is uncertain, but we like to think that the past is fixed and stable. Yet our understandings of the meanings of the past are always subject to reinterpretation. Because meanings are socially constructed, they can and do shift.

CHAPTER SIX

Economicization; or, Why Economists Get More Respect Than Sociologists

Consider all the people who seek to influence how we think about social problems. We have discussions with friends and family members, who share their views; social media sites forward everything from rumors to news stories; the Internet offers a forum for people to advance every conceivable point of view; and there are the more traditional media—books, articles, pamphlets, sermons, and so on. We are surrounded by claims about social problems, and we don't have enough time to digest more than a small minority of these claims. Which ones are worthy of our attention? And who makes those worthy claims?

In earlier chapters, we discussed some aspects of social-problems rhetoric, including the different ways we talk about similar problems (chapter 1), the sorts of evidence used to support claims about the future (chapter 3), and metaphors and other expressions used in future talk (chapter 4). What about the role of those who make claims, particularly experts, who are presumed to be especially qualified to speak? Definitions of which sorts of people should be considered experts shift over time. For example, during the Progressive Era, Protestant ministers played prominent, authoritative roles in campaigns to address a host of urban social issues, whereas today's clergy from the traditional mainline denominations have lost much of their ability to shape public opinion, although evangelical preachers' pronouncements seem able to influence how their flocks view social problems. In this chapter, I consider a similar shift in expert authority by examining the relative influence of two professions of social scientists. I argue that economists have been gaining greater attention in discussions of social problems, even as sociologists' ability to persuade a broad public seems to be slipping.

EXPERTS AS SOCIALLY DESIGNATED AUTHORITIES

Traditionally, professions have been defined in terms of their mastery of what are considered complex, important stocks of knowledge covering the law, medicine, or theology (Freidson 1986). This knowledge allowed professionals to interpret situations, understand problems, and devise solutions in ways that laypeople could not. Professionals had expertise.

Definitions of who qualifies as an expert vary across time and space. Different societies turn to all sorts of experts—shamans, traditional healers, midwives, and so on. Over the course of history, most experts probably acquired their knowledge by apprenticing themselves to a practitioner; but in recent centuries, formal training programs in law schools, medical schools, seminaries, and other professional schools have formed the basis for expertise.

When lots of people value a profession's expertise, it may be possible for practitioners of those professions to expand the domain their expertise covers. This is a reciprocal process: some members of a profession lay claim to new turf, arguing that they are qualified to interpret additional sorts of problems, even as some laypeople ratify those claims by turning to those experts to help deal with those problems.

In the sociological literature, medicalization is the most familiar example of this process. During the twentieth century, the authority of doctors expanded, thanks to the development of more effective treatments and the professionalization of medical education, licensing, and the like (Starr 1982). Medical treatments for many ailments improved dramatically: infectious diseases that were leading causes of death in 1900 now could be cured through antibiotics and improved sanitation, and new vaccines could prevent other diseases; mortality rates among young children and new mothers plunged, and overall life expectancies soared. People had more confidence in medical practitioners.

This growing confidence encouraged the expansion of the medical model—the vocabulary of disease, symptom, syndrome, and therapy—to cover a broader array of problems (Conrad and Schneider 1992; Conrad 2007). During traditional psychiatry's heyday in the middle decades of the twentieth century, there were claims that all manner of criminal and delinquent behaviors were forms of sickness that should be treated rather than punished. As the medical model was adopted by people outside traditional medical professions, those formerly called *drunkards* were relabeled *alcoholics,* and what had been a moral failing was now considered a disease. This thinking was extended by analogy to other conditions identified as addictions—drug addiction, food addiction, sex addiction, and the like. Students whose classroom performance fell short of expectations came to be understood as suffering from an array of learning disabilities, at least some of which could be treated through prescription drugs. Conditions that had once been considered normal physical variations—being of short stature, being over- or underweight, being bald, experiencing menopause, being dissatisfied which the shape of one's breasts or nose, being shy, and on and on—all became targets of medical intervention. And advances in biotechnology—genetic sequencing, brain scans, and such—invited new medical applications in the form of *biomedicalization* (Clarke et al. 2003).

To be sure, medicalization is not a one-way process. One can point to examples of sexual behaviors—such as masturbation, homosexuality, or kink (spanking, bondage, and related sexual practices)—that have been demedicalized (Gordon 2013; Lin 2017). Similarly, the midcentury readiness to view juvenile delinquency through a psychoanalytic lens seems to have dissipated. Still, when trying to understand what to do about problematic behaviors over the last century or more, a common response has been to turn to experts who adopt a medical model.

ECONOMICIZATION

While medicalization has been the focus of considerable sociological attention, it should not be seen as unique. Other professions, too, have gained or lost authority over time. *Economicization,* whereby economic models have been applied to an ever broader range of problems,* can be seen as a process parallel to medicalization, in that both involve expanding a profession's domain to encompass an ever broader range of subjects. In par-

* The term *economicization* has been used by other scholars (e.g., Chen 2002; Fourcade 2009). Still others prefer *economization* (Çalişkan and Callon 2009; Spring 2015). Neither term trips easily off the tongue, but I prefer the former because it seems to parallel *medicalization.*

ticular, at least part of the growth in economists' authority has come at the expense of sociologists; sociology has in effect ceded turf to the expertise of economists.

Obviously, the economy is a central social institution in every society. It was traditionally managed by government officials who oversaw coining and the realm's treasuries, and by private bankers and other moneylenders, rather than by people formally trained in the then-nonexistent discipline of economics. Protecting the nation's economy remains a central responsibility of today's federal government, but it is now taken for granted that professional economists play key roles in this process. The president has a Council of Economic Advisors, as well as cabinet posts for Treasury, Commerce, and Labor, departments that not only print money but also oversee the huge data-collection operations that track unemployment and other economic indicators; these departments employ many people trained in economics. Many of the government reports on economic indicators are issued quarterly or even monthly, and some are modified and updated as new information becomes available in efforts to improve their accuracy. In contrast, the data that sociologists tend to use are generated annually, or even less frequently (e.g., the decennial census), or derive from one-shot studies (Maier and Imazeki 2012).

Of course, businesses and financial markets are all about making money, and an array of media provide information for their participants, covering the economy and what are understood to be the practical applications of economic knowledge. In the era of print journalism, these media included newspapers such as the *Wall Street Journal,* magazines such as *Forbes* and *Business Week,* and countless specialized newsletters; much of this has now morphed and expanded into electronic media—the Bloomberg services and all sorts of specialized websites.

My quarrel is not with the applicability of economic knowledge to either the government's oversight of the economy or the business and financial worlds. What draws my attention is the recent interest in applying an economic perspective to an array of problems that have not traditionally been viewed as falling within the economist's purview and, in particular, to what are commonly called social problems (once considered the subject matter of sociology). Understanding these developments requires considering the history of economics as a social science.

THE EMERGENCE OF ECONOMICS

The rise of economics as a scholarly discipline—as opposed to the very long history of governments' and financiers' efforts to control money—is a relatively modern development. Adam Smith's *The Wealth of Nations* appeared in 1776, but it took more than a century for the discipline to take hold in academia. The American Economic Association was established in 1885, and the *Quarterly Journal of Economics* (the oldest English-language scholarly journal in the field) began publishing in 1886; the University of Chicago Press began publishing the *Journal of Political Economy* in 1892, only three years before it launched the *American Journal of Sociology*. The London School of Economics was founded in 1895.

Although people obviously have long been interested in understanding money, the scholarly discipline of economics emerged only near the end of the nineteenth century, more or less at the same time as sociology, anthropology, and political science (Furner 1975). Moreover, economics has long been suspect: Thomas Carlyle described it as "the dismal science" in 1849; its practitioners were derided, and many professional economists were touchy about this lack of respect: "Francis A. Walker was the first president of the [American Economic Association].... Over 100 years ago he felt the need to write a Sunday article on the low esteem in which political economy was then held. He found some pretty cogent reasons, most of which might hold today, with minor changes. For example, he thought the profession was too devoted to the abstraction of economic man, and too given to ignoring the importance of custom, law and institutions" (Solow 1985). Harry Truman, frustrated by economic advice phrased in terms of "On the one hand, ... but on the other hand, ..." famously wished for a one-handed economist. Complaints—and jokes—about economists have a long history.*

Sociologists find all of this familiar. Like economists, sociologists resent not receiving more respect. They, too, have long complained about being the subjects of dismissive remarks that characterize their writing as impenetrable jargon and their findings as mere common sense (Best 2003). Moreover, in contrast to the growing esteem enjoyed by economists, sociologists' stature seems to be in decline. Even before bookstores began to close their doors, their sociology sections were being recategorized as "Social Sciences" or "Cultural Studies." Authors were encouraged to avoid thinking of their work as sociological: "Sales will suffer ... if—horrors—a book is shelved away in Sociology—a catchall section for ambiguous titles, and the kiss of death for book sales" (Rinzler 2010).

In contrast, economics seems to be enjoying something of a boom in popular thinking. Economists are far more visible figures in the news media. For example, an analysis of the proportion of

---

* Economists are touchy about this (e.g., Mirowski 2010). They collect jokes about—and almost always at the expense of—economists (Economist-jokes.com 2016).

New York Times stories referring to different sorts of experts reports that "in recent years around one in 100 articles mention the term 'economist.' ... Far fewer articles mention the terms historian or psychologist, while sociologists, anthropologists and demographers rarely rate a mention" (Wolters 2015). In general, economists and other social scientists receive more attention than they used to: "Over the past 50 years, the pages of The Times have come to reflect an increasing fascination with the social sciences generally, and mentions of historians, psychologists and, to a lesser extent, sociologists have also risen. As social sciences have grown in importance, other sources of authority have lost market share. Priests were once more likely to be discussed in the pages of The Times than any of these social science celebrants, but today they are found far less often than either economists or historians, roughly on par with psychologists" (Wolters 2015). The same analyst tried to account for sociologists' failure to attract attention:

> Most striking is the poor showing of sociology, whose relevance to policy makers appears to be minimal, even though it focuses on many of our most pressing problems, including families, crime, education, aging, religion, community, inequality and poverty. Of course, sociologists, whose comparative advantage is in offering structural explanations, might point to the fact that their field has no equivalent of the business pages, that the president does not receive advice from a Council of Sociological Advisers, and that there's little demand from Wall Street for sociological insights.... More tellingly, as Orlando Patterson, a professor of sociology at Harvard, recently noted, sociology has limited impact even on issues central to the discipline. The most striking example he offered was that it appears that no sociologists were consulted in the deliberations surrounding President Obama's "My Brother's Keeper" initiative to combat the problems afflicting black youth, even as the insights of economists were sought. (Wolters 2015)

An alternative way of looking at the relative mentions of economics and sociology in recent years is displayed in figure 5, which tracks the ratio of *New York Times* articles containing the words *economist* or *economists* per article with the words *sociologist* or *sociologists,* across decades. A couple of things are clear. First, and this is hardly surprising, economists were mentioned far more often than sociologists in every decade. Second, sociologists received relatively more attention in the 1960s and 1970s than during other decades. This seems reasonable enough: the 1960s and 1970s were decades when a good deal of public attention was paid to social problems (think of the civil rights movement, the sexual revolution, the youth movement, the student movement, the women's movement, gay liberation, and so on). The press may have been more willing to acknowledge the cultural authority of sociologists during this period; articles referring to economists outnumbered those mentioning sociologists by only about five or seven to one, whereas in other decades the economists had roughly a ten-to-one advantage.

Economists are not just more likely to be mentioned by the media; they more often receive access to the media as a platform. Among public intellectuals—a term usually applied to professors and other experts who pontificate in the media—economists are more common than sociologists. There are not a lot of quantitative studies of public intellectuals, but Posner (2001) identified 546 such individuals who received frequent media attention from 1995 to 2000 and found that economists outnumbered sociologists 45 to 37 (in his classification, economists and sociologists ranked eighth and ninth respectively, behind lawyers (87), writers (78), journalists (63), historians and literature professors (57 each), philosophers (54), and political scientists (46). When Posner focused on the top 100 figures on his list, the gap widened to 10 economists (now the

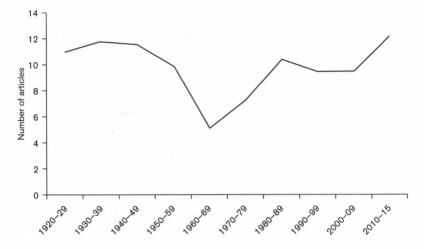

Figure 5. Number of articles in the *New York Times* mentioning economists per article mentioning sociologists, by decade, 1920–2015.

fourth most common category behind writers [34], lawyers [16], and journalists [15]) and only 2 sociologists. A few economists write regularly published columns in newspapers or magazines, such as Paul Krugman for the *New York Times* and Tim Harford for the *Financial Times;* so far as I know, no sociology professor has had equivalent, regular access to readers of print media. Studies of the authors of op-eds—individual columns written for the opinion pages of newspapers—find that, compared to sociologists, economists receive more of these opportunities to voice their views (Kowalchuk and McLaughlin 2009; Moseley and Teske 2011).*

The public visibility of economists is enhanced by there being a Nobel Prize in Economics. Although Alfred Nobel's

---

* Woods (2015) examines sociologists as op-ed writers in high-prestige newspapers and shows that while their presence on op-ed pages has increased, a larger share of those who write op-eds come from major universities.

original 1895 bequest established awards in chemistry, literature, medicine, physics, and peace to be administered by the Nobel Foundation, when Sweden's central bank launched the Nobel Memorial Prize in Economic Sciences in 1968, it was widely treated as the sixth Nobel Prize, and the awards are all presented at the same ceremony. Having attaining this signal honor gives Nobel laureates like Paul Krugman special authority when making statements (Lebaron 2006).

Economists do write fewer books than sociologists (Mochnacki, Segaert, and McLaughlin 2009), but their books are more likely to reach broad audiences. John Kenneth Galbraith, Milton Friedman, and most recently Thomas Piketty are academic economists who had books in the top place on the *New York Times* nonfiction best-seller list; sociology has attained that lofty height only through the services of journalist-interpreters, such as Vance Packard and Malcolm Gladwell. Moreover, a growing number of book titles aimed at trade audiences seek to show the power and utility of economic reasoning for understanding social problems, social policies, and even personal choices. Books such as Tim Harford's *The Underground Economist* (2006) and *The Underground Economist Strikes Back* (2014), and Steven D. Levitt and Stephen J. Dubner's best sellers *Freakonomics* (2005), *SuperFreakonomics* (2009), and *Think Like a Freak* (2014), are probably the best-known examples of this genre (Harford and Leavitt are economics professors). These books extend the domain of economic policy beyond traditional economic issues—whether taxes or interest rates should be raised or lowered and such. There have always been visible economists pontificating about economic policy—the roles once played by John Kenneth Galbraith and Milton Friedman are now filled by people such as Gary Becker, Francis Fukuyama, Paul Krugman, Robert Shiller, and Joseph Stiglitz. But as I discuss below, today's economists offer commentary on a much broader range of topics.

Economists are also more likely to be consulted by government officials. Economists are about twenty times more likely than sociologists to be mentioned in the *Congressional Record* (Wolters 2015); moreover, the language of economics plays an increasingly important role in policy debates. For example, Gormley (2012) tracked testimony at congressional hearings dealing with children's issues. He notes that during hearings on Lyndon Johnson's Great Society programs, witnesses tended to frame their remarks in moral or emotional terms along the lines of children being society's most vulnerable citizens, with the government having the responsibility for protecting and providing for those who lack other supports, and so supporting children's programs was presented as the right thing to do. In recent decades, the rhetoric of witnesses at congressional hearings has shifted, and the emphasis is now based on economic reasoning. Thus, advocates for children's programs argue that these programs more than pay for themselves, that when we compare the total costs of some program aimed at helping the young, against the total costs of dealing with the social problems the program is intended to prevent—kids who drop out of school, turn to drugs, get pregnant, and such—it will prove to be much cheaper to pay for this program than cover the costs society will face if young children don't receive this aid. Through such rhetoric, Congress is advised that they face a choice—pay something now, or pay far more in the future. Interestingly, Gormley is able to show that some of the same advocates, such as the Children's Defense Fund, switched their rhetoric from the moralizing they had offered in earlier decades to emphasizing costs and benefits in more recent times. Thus, economicization means that all sorts of policy claims are reworked into the language of economics.

It has probably always been the case that economists had greater public visibility than sociologists. Sociology probably reached its high-water mark in the thirty years following World War II, when society seemed to be undergoing particularly dramatic social changes. The press often turned to sociologists to interpret the meanings of beatniks and hippies, protesters, urban rioting, crime in the streets, and so on. Sociologists can be excused for suspecting that during the four-plus decades since 1975, their public presence has diminished, even as economics seems to be gaining greater influence.

THE APPEAL OF THE ECONOMIC MODEL

So, what accounts for the current enthusiasm for economics? Explanations for medicalization often begin by arguing that improvements in physicians' effectiveness in treating diseases accounts for the increased readiness to adopt the medical model for addressing a growing range of problems. No doubt economic knowledge, too, has improved, but this in itself does not seem to offer a sufficient explanation for the spread of economicization to the analysis of social problems. Three other factors also seem be at work.

An Easily Understood and Applicable Model

The first is that, while economics as a discipline is arcane, with a sophisticated, specialized vocabulary and complex methods that make its literature nearly impenetrable for noneconomists, its underlying principles are easily understood. That is, most people have no difficulty comprehending the notions that we live in a world of finite goods, and that people seek to maximize their satisfaction by making calculated choices that seem to lead to the optimal outcome. The basic interrelationships among of supply, demand, and price are probably also fairly widely understood, if only because there has been a campaign to promote economic literacy as a goal for education. By 2016, all fifty states listed economics in their K–12 educational standards, and twenty states (including California, Texas, Florida, and New York) required an economics course for high school graduation (Council for Economic Education 2016); each year about eighty-five thousand high school students take the advanced placement exam for macroeconomics, and fifty thousand take the microeconomics exam (College Board 2016).* U.S. textbook publishers estimate that between eight hundred thousand and a million undergraduates take an introductory sociology course each year, compared to about 1.2 million enrolled in introductory economics (Levitt 2016). Even if people have not had formal exposure to economics education, news reports about inflation, unemployment, and fluctuations in the stock market probably give lots of people at least a cursory sense of economic processes.†

We should not downplay the importance of a discipline offering a relatively straightforward, easily understood basic model.

---

* In comparison, no state requires high school sociology, and while the American Sociological Association established a task force in 2001 to do the groundwork for establishing an advanced placement course for sociology, there is still no sociology AP course.

† Note that popular understanding of supply and demand is a relatively recent development. One important variety of the preindustrial crowd was the bread riot, when the populace became outraged that bakers were charging more than the traditional price for a loaf of bread. The rioters did not understand, let alone acknowledge, that price increases might be a result of bad harvests reducing the supply of grain (Rudé 1964).

Consider a second example—the theory of evolution in biology.* While evolution is still controversial in some quarters, even its most devout critics understand its basic premise: that species evolve through a process of natural selection. It has proven easy for popularizers to translate the idea of evolution into all sorts of campaigns. Most notoriously, of course, evolution inspired the early-twentieth-century enthusiasm for eugenics—for social policies that would encourage breeding of what were regarded as better kinds of people while discouraging the multiplication of inferior ones.

More recently, a host of popular commentators have tried to explain puzzling human behaviors by arguing that the slow process of biological evolution has not kept up with rapid social changes. For instance, there is dietary advice based on the idea that prehistoric humans evolved bodies suited to eating naturally available foodstuffs, but that rapid changes in the food supply have led to all manner of unnatural, processed foods, and that people ought to adopt a paleo, or caveman, diet (Cordain 2002). Meanwhile, evolutionary psychology has inspired a popular literature aimed at understanding how biology underpins such diverse phenomena as politics, consumerism, and sexual attraction (Anonymous Conservative 2014; Etcoff 1999; Miller 2009). While very few people have formal training in either the basic science of evolution or evolutionary biology, there are plenty of claims that all sorts of social arrangements have their

* Both economic and evolutionary models have attracted some adherents within sociology to what they call, respectively, rational-choice theory and sociobiology. The American Sociological Association has sections on economic sociology, and on rationality and society, as well as on evolution, biology, and society, but neither orientation seems to be booming. According to *Sociological Abstracts,* journal articles with "sociobiolog*" in their titles peaked in the 1980s, those with titles mentioning "rational choice" in the 1990s.

roots in our evolutionary makeup, claims that can be understood by people with a cursory grasp of the perspective's basic
principles.

Just as the evolutionary model can easily be applied to all
types of social issues, so too can basic economic principles. There
is a kind of recipe here: take a troubling issue, apply a simple disciplinary framework, and—voila!—we can claim to have illumi-
nated the topic. In the case of economics, the key insight is that
people make what strike them as being optimizing choices—the
best option among the available alternatives. The typical line of
reasoning asks why some people make a troubling choice: Why
do some teenagers begin smoking? Or why do some industries
pollute? The analyst then explains that those people perceive
their options in such a way that the troubling choice seems optimal. The solution, of course, is to jigger the options, to make the
troubling choice seem less attractive, or to make what the analyst
sees as a preferred choice seem more attractive to people. This
tinkering may be quite overt, such as efforts to stamp out some
sort of crime by increasing legal penalties for those who wind up
being arrested. Or, it may be possible to structure choices in a
more subtle manner, so as to "nudge" more people to make the
analysts' preferred choices (Thaler and Sunstein 2009).

The behavior predicted by economic models depicts a world
of rational choices made by a figure once known as *economic man*
but now renamed *homo economicus* to avoid presumptive language
about gender. In economic theory, these idealized figures can be
counted on to behave in rational, predictable ways. Of course,
economists often find themselves dealing with the awkward fact
that real people don't behave in the rational manner their models predict. At the macro level, this is apparent when markets
irrationally get caught up in bubbles, in bidding up the value of

some good until the price suddenly collapses as many people try to get out all at once (Galbraith 1990). More recently, attention has focused on irrational, micro-decision-making. This is the domain of behavioral economics, in which researchers perform experiments that reveal their subjects' failures to attain pure rationality (Thaler 2015). Thus, many people commit the sunk-cost fallacy, in which they reason that their prior investments justify retaining or investing even more in what no longer seems to be a wise choice. There is now a large scholarly literature identifying ways in which individuals fall short of the homo economicus behavior predicted by traditional economic models. In turn, this research has been translated into popular books (Dobelli 2014; Lewis 2016; McRaney 2103) that catalog these errors, often naming them as fallacies, tendencies, or biases.

These ways people fall short of pure homo economicus rationality tend to be discussed one at a time. This makes it easy to ignore the ways these tendencies might seem to contradict one another. For example, Dobelli (2014) lists one hundred errors. Several of these involve people's tendencies to be overoptimistic, such as: *survivorship bias* ("People systematically overestimate their chances of success" [p. 3]); and the *overconfidence effect* ("you tend to overestimate your knowledge" [p. 45]). But then there are countervailing tendencies to be overpessimistic, such as: the *it'll-get-worse-before-it gets-better fallacy* (p. 33); or *loss aversion* ("The fear of losing something motivates people more than the prospect of gaining something of equal value" [p. 96]). Or consider the question of whether choices will display the *primacy effect* (favoring the first option) or the *recency effect* (favoring the last option; p. 218–20). All of these findings suggest that people's thinking may fall short of the sort of pure rationality envisioned by economics. And when applied after the fact, they make it possible to account for all manner of reasoning errors ("This must be why these people were too optimistic/pessimistic"), which is, of course, very different from being able to predict which errors will occur under given circumstances. Note, too, that behavioral economics tends to explain these errors in terms of flawed reasoning, so that the shortcomings belong to the realm of psychology—even evolutionary psychology. Thus, Dobelli (2014: 96) explains loss aversion: "People who were reckless or gung ho died before they could pass on their genes to the next generation. Those who remained, the cautious, survived. We are their descendants."

Both evolutionary psychology and behavioral economics meld a simply articulated model into the psychological literature. Thus, the sunk-cost fallacy and other, similar ways in which people fail to reason as economic theory predicts are understood to be psychological, rather than sociological, phenomena. The possibility that particular ways of thinking might be shaped by social context is rarely considered, let alone discounted.

Perceived Practical Value

A second advantage is that economics is popularly understood to be practical, in that it deals with something that most people consider important—the accumulation and protection of money. Understanding and handling money is central to business. Most people who receive formal training in finance, management, and the other academic disciplines taught in schools of business administration have taken at least a basic economics course or two, and economics is understood to provide the theoretical underpinning for their applied knowledge. In addition, of course, most individuals must learn to consider managing their personal finances as a necessary, extremely practical skill.

Like physics, economics features its own arcane terminology, less-than-intuitive concepts, and incomprehensible statistical methods that dramatically limit the number of people who can claim to understand its more refined claims. Yet many people are willing to defer to the expertise of the discipline's specialists, to assume that there must be something to it. This is abetted by the constant commentary by people offering economic-sounding interpretations of all sorts of events, such as fluctuations in the stock market or the general economy (Warner and Molotch 1993). There is a self-fulfilling prophecy here: people view economists as experts because they appear to understand important things, and they also believe that economic knowledge is important because everyone defers to economists.

However, claims for the practicality of economics are not simply a result of mystification. Economists argue that people make calculated rational choices. In the face of evidence that people often make choices that arguably end badly—such as marriages ending in divorce, or smokers winding up with lung cancer—behavioral economists suggest that these mistakes are patterned, that various cognitive processes lead to a set of errors in reasoning that can be categorized.

Intradisciplinary Debate

A third advantage is that economists are comfortable disagreeing with one another. The economic model can be applied to support a variety of arguments. Within American economics, people speak of debates between "freshwater" economists (a reference to the leading role played by economists from inland universities such as the University of Chicago, the University of Minnesota, and Carnegie Mellon University), who favor supply-side arguments, and "saltwater" economists (often found at universities on the east and west coasts, such as Harvard and Berkeley), who favor demand-side arguments. Put crudely, Republicans and conservatives tend to find support for their policy proposals from freshwater economists, while Democrats and liberals turn to saltwater economists for backing for their ideas. There is not one economic orthodoxy but an array of competing positions. This means that in virtually any policy debate, it is possible to find economists who are supporting very different positions. Thus, it is commonplace to find economists publishing op-eds that take opposing positions in prestigious forums that have very different editorial perspectives, for example, in both the conservative *Wall Street Journal* and the liberal *New York Times.*

Debate is probably good for economics, not only because it encourages a lively interchange within the discipline, but also because it means that advocates for lots of different causes might be able to find economic authorities who support their claims. People are less likely to ignore or dismiss economists' arguments as predictable. Instead, in the face of some economists taking a position at odds with their own, these people are more likely to roll out their own economists to offer support for their position.

All of these reasons—a simply understood model, a sense of that model's practical value, and lively debate within the profession—help explain the readiness with which people economicize, or adopt an economic model to frame lots of issues.

SOCIOLOGY'S DISADVANTAGES

When compared to economics, sociology seems to fair less well in the marketplace of ideas; it falls short on all three of the factors identified above.

The Absence of a Simple Model

First, sociology lacks the sort of simple models of mechanisms that give economics or evolutionary psychology their power. At bottom, sociologists argue that we are all innately social beings, and that our behaviors are affected by one another. Sociologists understand that this is a nontrivial insight, but it is not especially pointed, in that sociologists do not posit a single, easily understood way in which these effects are manifested. Depending on the topic, sociologists may focus on processes of socialization, on the power of culture, or on the influence of social structure; often, all of these are at work in shaping people's behavior.

In recent decades, American sociologists have become enamored of the idea of inequality. This represents something of a shift in emphasis. Surveys of the political orientations of professors in various academic disciplines have long found that sociology departments have one of the highest concentrations of self-identified liberals and/or Democrats on college campuses (Spaulding and Turner 1968; Ladd and Lipset 1975; Hamilton and Hargens 1993; Klein and Stern, 2005; Cardiff and Klein 2005; Gross and Simmons 2014). If anything, this homogeneity has increased, and sociology has moved further left: "over the last half-century the overwhelming movement has been in a critical direction" (Burawoy 2005: 7). In a sense, as sociologists have found it more difficult to reach a public audience, they increasingly have found themselves talking to one another in ideologically homogeneous conversations. For instance, the field that sociologists once called *social stratification* has always been central to the discipline. However, as noted in chapter 2, it has been reframed to emphasize inequality.

The problem with focusing intently on inequality is that it becomes predictable. The researchers say, in effect, "Look, over here! We can see inequality—circumstances that work to the disadvantage of those who are not well-to-do, straight, white males." Now this is certainly a reasonable finding. A basic form of sociological reasoning is to show patterns of difference between two groups (or, less often, unexpected similarities among apparently different groups). But recent sociologists' interpretations rarely offer much in the way of surprises. This is in sharp contrast to earlier decades, when sociologists' ability to reveal underlying social patterns seemed newsworthy. We have forgotten that *Life* magazine ran a set of Margaret Bourke-White photographs of social scenes in Muncie, Indiana, to accompany the release of the Lynds' classic study of social stratification, *Middletown in Transition* (Igo 2007). Those photos illustrated differences in the home furnishings and activities of Middletowners of different social classes. Similarly, sociology's all-time best-selling book— David Riesman's *The Lonely Crowd*—offered an interpretation of how American character had changed.* These were interesting, arresting ideas. Today, the journalist Malcolm Gladwell (2008) often offers interpretations of sociological works that seek to explain surprising patterns (e.g., Why do a disproportionate number of professional hockey players have birthdates between January and March?). When sociology attracts a large audience, it almost always is for having exposed social patterns that we fail to notice or that we take for granted.

In contrast, much contemporary sociology seems intent on demonstrating the various forms inequality takes. While it is

---

* On sociological best sellers, see Gans (1997); Longhofer, Golden and Baiocchi (2010).

certainly possible to identify new ways in which inequality is manifested (as when Gladwell writes about how birthdates lead to unequal prospects for hockey careers), or to provide better evidence for some familiar form of inequality, the focus on documenting inequality seems predictable, not particularly surprising, not something that attracts or holds public attention. The point is not that inequality is an unimportant or illegitimate topic for study—we clearly need analyses of inequality. But when sociology seems predictable, when it continually strikes the same note, it risks becoming boring and thereby less influential. Moreover, this predictability is related to confusion about sociology's core model. Unsure about just how sociologists reason, readers find it easy to equate their perspective with calls for social justice. Sociologists run the danger of being viewed as activists, rather than analysts. Even worse, they may seem to be scolds.

Apparently Unclear Practical Value

Sociology's second deficiency is that, unlike economics, it seems to lack practical value. In part, this reflects the discipline's long history of developing useful methodologies that then split off to become their own disciplines: examples include social work, management, public opinion polling, demography, and criminology—all applied disciplines with roots in sociology, which then broke away to find homes in other academic units (Best 2001). Sociologists tend to pride themselves on being a scholarly discipline that emphasizes theory over practicality, as a pure, rather than an applied, discipline. In comparison, economics and political science have managed to keep colleagues with applied interests within their disciplinary tents. While this may lead to some intradisciplinary bickering, this diversity probably makes those disciplines stronger. Meanwhile, sociology's devaluing of applied work to the point of driving it away probably encourages the many dismissive references to sociology as lacking practical value (e.g., "sociology is just common sense," "that's all fine in theory," etc.)

There is an irony here. Sociology has been remarkably successful as a wellspring for concepts that emigrate into mainstream conversations. Lots of people unthinkingly use terms like *status symbol, charisma, role model,* and *stigma*—terms that have their modern roots in sociological analyses, although the widespread popularization of these concepts often causes those origins to be forgotten. Like Molière's *bourgeois gentilhomme* who was shocked to learn he'd been speaking prose, many members of the public might be astonished to learn that they have been speaking—and thinking—sociologically without ever knowing it. Sociology is considered useless at least in part because whenever sociological ideas are deemed useful, their connections to sociology become forgotten.

In addition, the discipline's focus on inequality makes it easy to assume that sociology is primarily useful for activists who might want to challenge social injustice. It is less clear what sociology offers those who might want to apply a sociological perspective to other topics. The broader value of a sociological perspective is most often communicated to the larger public by Malcolm Gladwell and other interpreters from outside the discipline.

The Costs of Ideological Homogeneity

The third problem is that sociologists tend to speak with one voice. Take just one dramatic example from the decades of research studies on the political orientations of academics in different disciplines. A 2005 study of voter-registration records for faculty at eleven California colleges and universities found that among sociologists, registered Democrats outnumbered Republicans 44 to 1 (Cardiff and Klein 2005). In comparison, while researchers consistently find that economics professors also are more likely to describe themselves as liberals and Democrats, the margin is much less overwhelming. The California study, for instance, found 2.8 registered Democrats for every Republican among economics professors. While academic economists are most likely to be liberals, the research generally finds that something like one-fifth to one-quarter are conservatives. This division should not be unexpected, given those debates between the freshwater and saltwater schools.

The near-unanimity of liberalism among sociologists is reflected in the discipline's recent emphasis on inequality, but it has other, more important consequences. It discourages debate or even expressions of difference among sociologists and helps explain the sanctimonious, scolding tones adopted by some sociologists. If you can assume that virtually everyone in a discipline agrees, it is easy to assume that this consensus refers to some larger truth—the way things are—rather than sociologists' shared ideology. And, being confident in the righteousness of one's cause offers a license to speak dismissively about those who hold other views. As social psychologists have long understood, many people wilt in the face of overwhelming criticism; they are reluctant to speak out. But intimations of moral superiority are unlikely to attract listeners—let alone adherents—among the public. Even worse, sociologists' spectrum of positions, spanning all the way from very-left to solidly liberal, makes what sociologists have to say on most topics seem relatively predictable. In contrast to the way people on different sides of policy debates are likely to try to find support from economists, individuals who consider themselves more conservative on some issue may not bother to ask what sociologists have to say on the topic.

For the most part, contemporary sociologists—like economists—are caught up in producing sophisticated statistical analyses impossible for the general public—or, in fact, most sociologists—to appreciate. But when they do address public issues, economists have different, sometimes surprising things to say, while sociologists tend to be predictably denouncing inequality. Michael Burawoy's (2005: 25) call for public sociology received considerable attention from sociologists; but while he acknowledged that public sociology might take various forms, he argued for the importance of "a critically disposed public sociology" in which scholar activists might invoke sociology in the cause of social justice. But of course, joining this cause—and thinking of public sociology in these terms—reinforces the predictability of what sociologists say. And being predictable—particularly if what is predictable is delivering a stern talking-to—makes it less likely that people will take an interest in what sociologists have to say on a given topic.

In short, when compared to economics, sociology lacks a simple, easily understood model of social life that can be used to investigate all manner of topics, the discipline's practical value is less apparent, and its political homogeneity makes it seem predictable. No wonder sociologists seem to be increasingly marginalized in the public square.

CONCLUSION

Obviously, it is possible to exaggerate the scale of economics' triumph and sociology's plight. We don't need to assume that there is some finite amount of social authority, that if one profession's public standing rises, another's inevitably falls by an equal amount. Still, some of the rise of medicalization seems to have come at the expense of religious authorities, although this hardly means that religion has lost all of its power to shape public debates. And mainstream medicine has its rivals in chiropractic, acupuncture, homeopathy, and various other alternative models for healing, just as religion offers many competing interpretations. No discipline's experts ever speak in a single authoritative voice, at least not in large, complex societies.

Sociologists of social problems use the metaphor of the marketplace to portray advocates trying to draw attention to particular troubling conditions as vendors who must compete for the attention of the public, the press, and policy makers (Best 2017; Hilgartner and Bosk 1988). But this is not just a competition among claims: it is also a competition among claimsmakers who evoke different sorts of authority. Some ground their claims in their own victimization and the harms they have suffered, some in various moral or ideological principles, and still others in some type of professional expertise. Over time, the relative fortunes of these different kinds of claimsmakers shift. So we can think of medicalization—or economicization—as a process by which the claims of a particular authoritative perspective come to advance more successfully.

Although the literature on medicalization has been extremely useful, it builds upon a single case—medicine's growing authority. Studying economicization invites comparisons with a second case of a profession having greater success in promoting its interpretation of social problems. Both cases involve professions with huge literatures grounded in specialized vocabularies and methodologies that may strike laypeople as impenetrable; most people who defer to these experts must take on faith that they know what they're doing. Understanding how the relative authority of professions shifts over time cannot rest on a single case; it requires thinking comparatively across different cases.

The histories of academic disciplines—and of all institutions that claim expertise—seem simple and consistent only when they are viewed from a great distance. Seen up close, they seem filled with competition, even conflict. Schools of thought emerge, centered on particular ideas (variously termed doctrines or theories) or practices (conventions or methodologies). Some catch on swiftly; others only slowly. Some remain influential, while others fall away. Although there is always a tendency to assume that what strikes us as important will have lasting value, history teaches that the debates that rage today may be little remembered tomorrow.

The sociological perspective naturally appeals to our discipline's members; we are its self-selected followers. It is easy to be a little impatient, a little frustrated with those who don't seem to appreciate sociology's value. But we compete in a marketplace of ideas, and no one is obliged to buy our wares. If sociology's influence seems to be receding, we ought to look to what economics—another social science, whose impact seems to be growing—is doing differently. There are reasons why people pay attention to economists: economics has an easily understood model that can be adapted to advance all manner of claims; economists sometimes say surprising, interesting things. Sociologists are never going to be able to reduce sociology to a simple model, but our thinking could become less predictable. In a discipline where people insist that diversity is a strength, sociologists might consider welcoming a range of views.

Afterword

The Future of American Nightmares

Our track record is clear: Americans find things to worry about. No doubt all people throughout history have had things that worried them, but a lot of the fears in traditional societies must have seemed fairly familiar—worrying about a bad harvest, getting sick, and so on.

In contrast, Americans' worries have continually morphed; we have always been able to find lots of new things to fear. We live, my students like to tell me, in a rapidly changing world. And we do. But Americans two hundred years ago had that same sense that the world was changing fast—and they were right. There were those newfangled railroads that moved people at unimaginable speeds, and the country was spreading westward into new and sometimes astonishingly different territory. And—but you get the idea. At every point in American history, people could wonder at the rapid changes in their world, even as they discovered new concerns about what those changes might mean for the future.

We remain susceptible to these concerns. Donald Trump's successful presidential campaign relied heavily on rhetoric about threats menacing America—and other politicians' failure to address them. These fears resonated with some voters, and in turn Trump's many critics portrayed that response as frightening. While we might imagine that a better-educated population with greater access to information might be better able to evaluate claims about American Nightmares, there are countervailing trends. There is stiff competition for attention in the online world, and those who shout loudest find it easier to be heard. There is little advantage to making restrained, carefully reasoned analyses in such an environment. This is particularly true because the audience is segmented by race, class, gender, ideology, religion, sexual preference, and other variables, and people find it easy to congregate among and listen to those who share their views—and their worries.

Often, those worries tap into standard themes. Consider how Americans at different points in our history—including today—would have filled in the blanks in these sentences:

- I think we ought to worry about these new immigrants from _____; I don't think they'll ever fit in and become good Americans.
- I think we ought to worry about these kids today and the way they've started to _____; I don't think they'll grow up to be good adults.
- I think we ought to worry about people who believe _____; I think they're too different.

It is easy to get distracted by, say, worrying about how youths are using the newest smartphone app and to forget about the previous generations of adults who worried—at least as much—about how their kids might be permanently harmed by their exposure to whatever was the newest form of popular culture; we lose sight of the once-intense concerns over dime novels, nickelodeons, and jazz.* Worrying about the corruption of youth is a standard theme in American social history. It is just one of our major cultural fault lines—underlying themes that spark our fears, even if the particulars shift over time. Our newest concerns always seem unprecedented: we forget the worries of our predecessors, if only because rosy-hued nostalgia turns the remembered past into a seemingly innocent, trouble-free time. It must have been that way; after all, everything turned out pretty well, so we can tell ourselves that those people really didn't have much to worry them.

There is nothing new about American Nightmares, then. Americans have been having them since before witches bedeviled Salem. Like an individual caught up in an ordinary nightmare, large sections of society can become anxious, and only time can dissipate the anxiety. When we awaken from a nightmare, we can dismiss our fears. That was just a bad dream. But just as our dreams tap into our personal fears in ways that make sense to us, so do we talk about American Nightmares using rhetoric that is socially resonant. We choose language that makes the putative objects of our fears—such as those kids using that new app—into a disturbing threat. This threat endangers not just our own kids (who, after all, are good kids who have been raised to know better) but also all those other kids who may not have been as well-raised—and what will happen when all those endangered kids become the adults in our society's future. Notice the easy transition from worrying about today's young to

* Several scholars have described historical moral panics regarding youth and new forms of popular culture (Springhall 1998; Sternheimer 2015; Thiel-Stern 2014).

worrying about America's future; in this way, we can imagine even small problems as having huge implications for what may come. And it may take time to awaken from our collective American Nightmares to discover that, yet again, our worries were overblown.

By most measures, the American experiment has gone remarkably well. Compared to other human societies across time and space, our population is astonishingly healthy (think average life expectancy), wealthy (standard of living), and wise (at least, as measured in average years of schooling). There have been millions of people who have improved their lots by coming to America—millions of American Dreams fulfilled to one degree or another.

And yet, it is easy to characterize the glass as half empty. We can always imagine being even healthier, wealthier, and wiser. Even if many people have fulfilled some of their aspirations, achieved some version of their personal American Dreams, it remains possible to point to all the people who fell short, who did not see all of their dreams fulfilled. (And sociologists, of course, are adept at identifying social patterns in these disappointments, at discovering that those who are disadvantaged are most vulnerable to further disappointments.) It is always possible to make claims about new (and not-so-new) social problems.

This is not to discount the validity of those claims. So long as we hold perfection as a standard, it is certain that we will fall short: some people will indeed die in troubling ways, just as others will suffer lesser harms. Americans have seen lots of progress, yet it is always possible to insist we could do better, much as it is also possible to argue that what looks like progress is an illusion. (The fact that more people have more formal schooling doesn't necessarily mean that we're getting wiser. Our ancestors may have had less book learning, but they had more real wisdom.) If every cloud has a silver lining, there is also the prospect that every sunny day increases our risk of skin cancer.

The chapters in this book make a case for stepping back from our worries and thinking critically about them. Their topics may seem diverse, even unrelated. What do popular hazards have to do with the American Dream, or with predictions of catastrophes, with future talk, the Confederate battle flag, or economicization? But there are common themes that run through these chapters.

The first concerns the special challenges of worrying about the future. While trying to anticipate and avoid problems that lie ahead is a perfectly sensible activity, all predictions are subject to skepticism: given that no one can know the future for certain, why should we believe a specific forecast? In retrospect, skeptics were often right. The world did not end on Y2K, or on December 21, 2012. Similarly, the population bomb failed to explode, and moving pictures (like all of the innovations in popular culture that preceded and followed them) did not ruin the next generation of young people. The list of apocalyptic predictions that failed to come true is very long.

Still, advocates must confront and overcome this inevitable skepticism. While terrible events—say, a dramatic bridge collapse—can capture public attention and sympathy, raising concern requires arguing that this incident needs to be understood as an instance of a larger, impending problem: if we don't act now to address our failing infrastructure, there will be more, possibly much worse, crises in the future. Even though such predictions aren't always right, we need to plan for what seems likely to happen. And because it can be hard to get people to focus calmly on the future, alarmist language becomes an attractive tactic for raising concern.

This leads to the book's second theme, the importance of rhetoric, of the words used to persuade people that they ought to worry. This involves making those always-subject-to-skepticism predictions seem convincing and compelling, so that the listeners are moved to take action. Those who forecast the future—from an evangelist giving a time-certain date for the Second Coming, to climate scientists presenting the results of their computer models—often complain that it is hard to get people to pay attention to their urgent warnings. Whether people listen to a prediction, accept it, and act upon it depends not just on the nature of the warning but also on how that warning is presented.

The book's third theme concerns sociology's role in thinking about American Nightmares. Certainly, as a sociologist, I am convinced that our discipline has a great deal to offer. At the same time, I am dismayed that sociology too often seems predictable and, as a result, has increasing difficulty influencing the public conversation about social problems. I suppose I am calling for an expanded sociological mandate.

There are now many hundreds of case studies of social problems being constructed. A single case study requires a manageable amount of work that can lead to a thesis or an article in a professional journal, and many analysts have mastered the skills required to conduct these case studies. But as the constructionist literature grows, it becomes clear that building a great mass of cases studies has had costs as well as benefits (Best 2015).

In particular, cases studies—by definition—focus narrowly on the particulars of the case under consideration. This makes it harder to see how a case relates to others, how it might be similar to—or different from—other cases. All of the chapters in this book call for looking beyond single cases: Chapter 1 calls for sociologists to recognize a common underlying policy issue (how to balance an activity's popularity with its risks) that runs through many, seemingly unrelated and very different social problems. Chapter 2 examines how various commentators—including sociologists—have constructed the American Dream as a social problem. Chapter 3 compares three very different projections of future catastrophes and tries to explain why they've elicited very different policy reactions. Chapter 4 shows that the same metaphors are used to support all manner of visions of the future. Chapter 5 considers how constructions of the past are fluid. And chapter 6 contrasts the relative success of two social sciences in attracting popular support for their analyses. Each of these chapters argues that something is to be gained by moving beyond case studies and by comparing instances of social-problem construction.

Moving beyond particular cases in favor of a broader perspective can make our American Nightmares seem less alarming. Contemporary culture involves an extraordinary competition for people's attention. Fifty years ago, a typical American home had a telephone line, subscriptions to a newspaper and perhaps a few magazines, and a television set that received broadcasts from a small number of local stations—and commentators worried that all of these mass media might lead to a mass society where every individual was receiving the same messages and, in the process, becoming just like everyone else. Today, those worries seem laughable. Individuals have devices—televisions that offer not just hundreds of channels but also access to the Internet, to say nothing of an array of smartphones, computers, and so on. There is an essentially infinite amount of content, and few people consume precisely the same set of messages. Today's commentators complain that rather than focusing on one thing, people spend much of their time just scanning for new information.

This means that those who want to get people to focus on something need to grab and hold their attention. This is true for all manner of activities, from individuals trying to attract likes to their Facebook posts, to television broadcasters competing for viewers, to activists trying to arouse concern for their causes. These competitions favor those whose messages can grab and hold an audience, and making people scared or outraged is among the tried-and-true methods of doing this. Moderation and keeping things in perspective make one's claims less competitive. This theme, too, runs through this book's chapters: popular hazards must be portrayed as terribly dangerous; the American Dream is not so much an ideal as a force that ruins people's lives; predictions about the future must focus on calamity; and so on.

Sociologists—like other commentators—can get caught up in exposing particular issues and exaggerating their dangers, even to the point that they construct yet additional American Nightmares. Their concerns may be serious and sincere. Still, it can't hurt to step back from the urgency about whatever the anxiety of the day may be, to consider the record of such concerns across time and space.

References

Adams, James Truslow. (1931) 1941. *The Epic of America*. Garden City, NY: Blue Ribbon Books.

Alessi, Scott. 2012. "Capitol Gains: New Strategies Are Paying Off for the Pro-life Movement." *U.S. Catholic* 77 (January): 26–29.

Altman, Lawrence K. 1982. "New Homosexual Disorder Worries Health Officials." *New York Times*, May 11.

Andersen, Margaret, and Howard F. Taylor. 2011. *Sociology: The Essentials*. 6th ed. Belmont, CA: Wadsworth.

Anderson, Nick. 2015. "William and Mary Drops a Confederate Emblem and Moves a Plaque." *Washington Post Blogs*, August 14. www.washingtonpost.com/news/grade-point/wp/2015/08/14/william-mary-drops-a-confederate-emblem-and-moves-a-plaque/.

Anonymous Conservative. 2014. *The Evolutionary Psychology behind Politics: How Conservatism and Liberalism Evolved within Humans*. McClenny, FL: Federalist Publications.

Apuzzo, Matt. 2003. "Connecticut Supreme Court Says Fetus Is Body Part." Associated Press, May 7.

Argüelles, José. 1987. *The Mayan Factor: Path beyond Technology*. Santa Fe, NM: Bear.

Associated Press. 2003. "Excerpt from Santorum Interview." *USA Today*, April 23. http://usatoday30.usatoday.com/news/washington /2003–04–23-santorum-excerpt_x.htm.

Attarian, John. 2002. *Social Security: False Consciousness and Crisis*. New Brunswick, NJ: Transaction.

Auten, Gerald, and Geoffrey Gee. 2009. "Income Mobility in the United States: New Evidence from Income Tax Data." *National Tax Journal* 62: 301–28.

Bacon, Heather. 2008. "Cleveland 20 Years On: What Have We Learned about Intervening in Child Sexual Abuse?" *Child Abuse Review* 17: 215–29.

Baer, Susan. 2016. "Racism Chiseled on Our Walls—and the Fight to Erase It." CNN.com, February 15. www.cnn.com/2016/02/15/politics /presidents-day-woodrow-wilson/.

Banks, Emily, et al. 2015. "Tobacco Smoking and All-Cause Mortality in a Large Australian Cohort Study: Findings from a Mature Epidemic with Current Low Smoking Prevalence." *BMC Medicine* 13:38. http://bmcmedicine.biomedcentral.com/articles/10.1186/s12916–015–0281-z.

Bartow, Paul. 2015. "The Growing Threat of Historical Presentism." *AEIdeas* (American Enterprise Institute), December 10. www.aei .org/publication/the-growing-threat-of-historical-presentism/.

Bates, Timothy Mason. 1997. *Race, Self-Employment, and Upward Mobility: An Illusive American Dream*. Washington, DC: Woodrow Wilson Center Press.

Becker, Howard S. 1995. "The Power of Inertia." *Qualitative Sociology* 18: 301–9.

Béland, Daniel. 2005. *Social Security: History and Politics from the New Deal to the Privatization Debate*. Lawrence: University Press of Kansas.

Bell, Larry. 2013. "The Slippery Slope of Gun Control: Time to Stand on Firm Ground." *Forbes.com*, January 15. www.forbes.com/sites /larrybell/2013/01/15/the-slippery-slope-of-gun-control-time-to-stand-on-firm-ground/#42a657b210ac.

Beller, Emily, and Michael Hout. 2006. "Intergenerational Social Mobility: The United States in Comparative Perspective." *Future of Children* 16 (2): 19–36.

Bennett, William J., John J. DiIulio, and John P. Walters. 1996. *Body Count: Moral Poverty … and How to Win America's War against Crime and Drugs*. New York: Simon and Schuster.

Bennett, William J., and Robert A. White. 2015. *Going to Pot: Why the Rush to Legalize Marijuana Is Harming America*. New York: Center Street.

Berg, A. Scott. 2013. *Wilson*. New York: Putnam's.

Best, Joel. 1990. *Threatened Children: Rhetoric and Concern about Child-Victims*. Chicago: University of Chicago Press.

———. 2001. "Giving It Away: The Ironies of Sociology's Place in Academia." *American Sociologist* 32 (Spring): 107–13.

———. 2003. "Killing the Messenger: The Social Problems of Sociology." *Social Problems* 50: 1–13.

———. 2011a. "If This Goes On … : The Rhetorical Construction of Future Problems." In *Bending Opinion: Essays on Persuasion in the Public Domain*, edited by Ton van Haaften, Henrike Jansen, Jaap de Jong, and Willem Koetsenruijter, 203–17. Leiden, Netherlands: Leiden University Press.

———. 2011b. "What's New? What's Normal?" *Sociological Forum* 26: 790–95.

———. 2012. *Damned Lies and Statistics: Untangling Numbers from the Media, Politicians, and Activists*. Updated ed. Berkeley: University of California Press.

———. 2015. "Beyond Case Studies: Expanding the Constructionist Framework for Social Problems Research." *Qualitative Sociology Review* 11 (April): 18–33.

———. 2017. *Social Problems*. 3rd ed. New York: Norton.

Bowman, Karlyn, Jennifer Marsico, and Heather Sims. 2014. *Is the American Dream Alive? Examining Americans' Attitudes*. American Enterprise Institute, December. www.aei.org/wp-content/uploads/2014/12/Is-the-American-Dream-Alive_Dec2014.pdf.

Brady Center to Prevent Gun Violence. 2016. "Risks of Having a Gun in the Home." www.bradycampaign.org/risks-of-having-a-gun-in-the-home.

Brekke, Kira. 2015. "Polyamorous Attorney Agrees SCOTUS Decision Could Lead to Group Marriage." *Huffington Post*, July 4. www

.huffingtonpost.com/2015/07/04/same-sex-marriage-polygamy_n_
7705744.html.

Brinkerhoff, David B., Lynn K. White, Suzanne T. Ortega, and Rose
Weitz. 2011. *Essentials of Sociology*. 8th ed. Belmont, CA: Wadsworth.

Brown, Michael. 2012. "Here Comes Incest, Just as Predicted." *Townhall.
com*, September 11. http://townhall.com/columnists/michaelbrown
/2012/09/11/here_comes_incest_just_as_predicted.

Brown, Thomas J. 2011. "The Confederate Battle Flag and the Deser-
tion of the Lost Cause Tradition." In *Remixing the Civil War: Medita-
tions on the Sesquicentennial*, edited by Thomas J. Brown, 37–72. Baltimore, MD: Johns Hopkins University Press.

Burawoy, Michael. 2005. "For Public Sociology." *American Sociological
Review* 70: 4–28.

Bush, Melanie E.L., and Roderick D. Bush. 2015. *Tensions in the American
Dream: Rhetoric, Reverie, or Reality*. Philadelphia, PA: Temple University Press.

Cahill, Courtney Megan. 2005. "Same-Sex Marriage, Slippery Slope
Rhetoric, and the Politics of Disgust: A Critical Perspective on
Contemporary Family Discourse and the Incest Taboo." *Northwest-
ern University Law Review* 99: 1543–611.

Çalişkan, Koray, and Michael Callon. 2009. "Economization, Part 1:
Shifting Attention from the Economy towards Processes of Economization." *Economy and Society*, 38: 369–98.

Cardiff, Christopher F., and Daniel B. Klein. 2005. "Faculty Partisan
Affiliations in All Disciplines: A Voter-Registration Study." *Critical
Review* 17: 237–55.

Census Bureau. 2016. *Current Population Survey, 2016 Annual Social and
Economic Supplement*. www.census.gov/data/tables/time-series/demo
/income-poverty/cps-hinc/hinc-05.2015.html.

Center for Behavioral Health Statistics and Quality. 2010. "Treatment
Episode Data Set (TEDS), 1998–2008." Department of Health
and Human Services. December. wwwdasis.samhsa.gov/teds08
/TEDS2k8Sweb.pdf.

Centers for Disease Control and Prevention. 2012. "Drowning: United
States, 2005–2009." *Morbidity and Mortality Weekly Report*. May 18.
www.cdc.gov/mmwr/preview/mmwrhtml/mm6119a4.htm#tab.

―――. 2014. "Nonfatal Injury Reports, 2001–2013" (WISQARS [Web-Based Injury Statistics Query and Reporting System]). www.cdc.gov/injurt/wisqars/index.html.

―――. 2015a. "All Injuries." www.cdc.gov/nchs/fastats/injury.htm.

―――. 2015b. "Bicycle Safety." www.cdc.gov/motorvehiclesafety/bicycle/.

―――. 2015c. "Cigarette Smoking in the United States." www.cdc.gov/tobacco/campaign/tips/resources/data/cigarette-smoking-in-united-states.html.

Chen, Sheying. 2002. "Economic Reform and Social Change in China: Past, Present, and Future of the Economic State." *International Journal of Politics, Culture and Society* 15: 569–89.

Chen, Victor. 2015. *Cut Loose: Joblessness and Hopelessness in an Unfair Economy.* Berkeley: University of California Press.

Chetty, Raj, David Grusky, Maximilian Hell, Nathaniel Hendren, Robert Manduca, and Jimmy Narang. 2016. "The Fading American Dream: Trends in Absolute Income Mobility since 1940." NBER Working Paper 22910. National Bureau of Economic Research. December. www.equality-of-opportunity.org/papers/abs_mobility_paper.pdf.

Chinoy, Ely. 1955. *Automobile Workers and the American Dream.* Garden City, NJ: Doubleday.

Citizens Against Legalizing Marijuana (CALM). 2015a. "Marijuana Is Dangerous and It Kills." August 14. http://calmusa.org/calmcablog/2015/8/14/yamsyfecbdslez7rr6ks5u4kynwosi.

―――. 2015b. "Marijuana Is Devastating to Youth." August 16. http://calmusa.org/calmcablog/2015/8/16/marijuana-is-devastating-to-youth.

―――. 2015c. "The Myths of Marijuana." August 14. http://calmusa.org/calmcablog/2015/8/14/the-myths-of-marijuana.

―――. 2015d. "Smoked Marijuana Jeopardizes the Physical and Mental Health of Everyone." August 16. http://calmusa.org/calmcablog/2015/8/16/qjzkw9808wqvo84zixffudezao59fw.

Clarke, Adele E., Janet K. Shim, Laura Mamo, Jennifer Ruth Fosket, and Jennifer R. Fishman. 2003. "Biomedicalization: Technoscientific Transformations of Health, Illness, and U.S. Biomedicine." *American Sociological Review* 68: 161–94.

Clinton, Hillary. 2016. "The American Dream Is Alive Rally." May 17. www.youtube.com/watch?v=uzTnfcgN_Zg.

Cole, David. 2016. "Race and Renaming: A Talk with Peter Salovey, President of Yale." *New York Review of Books* 63 (June 9): 42–44.

College Board. 2016. "AP Central: AP Macroeconomics and AP Microeconomics Frequently Asked Questions." http://apcentral.collegeboard.com/apc/public/courses/220356.html.

Comay, Laura B., and Barbara Salazar Torreon. 2015. "Display of the Confederate Flag at Federal Cemeteries." *CRS Insights,* July 10. www.fas.org/sgp/crs/misc/IN10313.pdf.

Connecticut Historical Society. 2016. "Yale Civil War Memorial." Accessed May 14. https://chs.org/finding_aides/ransom/077.htm.

Conrad, Peter. 2007. *The Medicalization of Society: On the Transformation of Human Conditions into Treatable Disorders.* Baltimore, MD: Johns Hopkins University Press.

Conrad, Peter, and Joseph W. Schneider. 1992. *Deviance and Medicalization: From Badness to Sickness.* Expanded ed. Philadelphia, PA: Temple University Press.

Cook, Robert J. 2007. *Troubled Commemoration: The American Civil War Centennial, 1961–1965.* Baton Rouge: Louisiana State University Press.

Cooper, Christopher A., and H. Gibbs Knotts. 2006. "Region, Race, and Support for the South Carolina Confederate Flags." *Social Science Quarterly* 87: 142–54.

Cooper, Henry F. 2016. "Near a Tipping Point?" *High Frontier,* April 19. http://highfrontier.org/april-19–2016-near-a-tipping-point/.

Corcoran, M. 1995. "Rags to Rags: Poverty and Mobility in the United States." *Annual Review of Sociology* 21: 237–67.

Cordain, Loren. 2002. *The Paleo Diet: Lose Weight and Get Healthy by Eating the Foods You Were Designed to Eat.* New York: Wiley.

Coski, John M. 2005. *The Confederate Battle Flag: America's Most Embattled Emblem.* Cambridge, MA: Harvard University Press.

Council for Economic Education. 2016. *Survey of the States: Economics and Personal Finance Education in Our Nation's Schools, 2016.* New York: Council for Economic Education. http://councilforeconed.org/wp/wp-content/uploads/2016/02/sos-16-final.pdf.

Cullen, Jim. 2003. *The American Dream: A Short History of an Idea That Shaped a Nation*. New York: Oxford University Press.

Dahlgren, Peter. 2012. "Public Intellectuals, Online Media, and Public Spheres: Current Realignments." *International Journal of Politics, Culture, and Society* 25: 95–110.

Daipha, Phaedra. 2015. *Masters of Uncertainty: Weather Forecasters and the Quest for Ground Truth*. Chicago: University of Chicago Press.

Davidai, Shai, and Thomas Gilovich. 2015. "Building a More Mobile America—One Income Quintile at a Time." *Perspectives on Psychological Science* 10: 60–71.

Davis, Mike. 1986. *Prisoners of the American Dream: Politics and Economy in the History of the US Working Class*. London: Verso.

DeJong, William, and Jason Blanchette. 2014. "Case Closed: Research Evidence on the Positive Public Health Impact of the Age 21 Minimum Legal Drinking Age in the United States." *Journal of Studies on Alcohol and Drugs,* supplement, 17: 108–15.

Del Rosso, Jared. 2015. *Talking about Torture: How Political Discourse Shapes the Debate*. New York: Columbia University Press.

DeMause, Lloyd. 1974. "The Evolution of Childhood." In *The History of Childhood,* edited by Lloyd deMause, 1–73. New York: Psychohistory Press.

Derschowitz, Jessica. 2015. "Warner Bros. Nixing Dukes of Hazzard General Lee Toys over Confederate Flag." *EW.com,* June 24. www.ew.com/article/2015/06/24/dukes-hazzard-general-lee-confederate-flag.

Dobelli, Rolf. 2014. *The Art of Thinking Clearly*. New York: Harper.

DogsBite.org. 2015. "2011 Dog Bite Fatalities." www.dogsbite.org/dog-bite-statistics-fatalities-2011.php.

Dolan, Eric W. 2012. "Jon Stewart Mocks 'Slippery Sodomy Slope Scalia.'" RawStory.com, December 13. www.rawstory.com/2012/12/jon-stewart-mocks-slippery-sodomy-slope-scalia/.

Dunn, Jennifer L. 2010. *Judging Victims: Why We Stigmatize Survivors, and How They Reclaim Respect*. Boulder, CO: Lynne Rienner.

Economistjokes.com. 2016. "The Jokes about Economists and Economics." Accessed September 5. www.economistjokes.com/jokes.

Edmondson, Brad. 2011. "The U.S. Bicycle Market: A Trend Overview." Gluskin Townley Group. www.gluskintownleygroup.com/downloads /The%20US%20Bicycle%20Market%20-%20A%20Trend%20Overview%20Report.pdf.

Ehrenreich, Barbara. 2005. *Bait and Switch: The (Futile) Pursuit of the American Dream*. New York: Metropolitan Books.

Ellis, Abraham. 1971. *The Social Security Fraud*. New Rochelle, NY: Arlington.

Ellis, Charles D., Alicia H. Munnell, and Andrew D. Eschtruth. 2014. *Falling Short: The Coming Retirement Crisis and What to Do about It*. New York: Oxford University Press.

Etcoff, Nancy. 1999. *Survival of the Prettiest: The Science of Beauty*. New York: Doubleday.

Farley, John E. 1998. *Earthquake Fears, Predictions, and Preparations in Mid-America*. Carbondale: Southern Illinois University Press.

Farley, Melissa, and Victor Malarek. 2008. "The Myth of Victimless Crime." *New York Times,* March 12.

Fendrick, Sabrina. 2014. "Here's What Colorado Looks Like 6 Months into Legalization." NORML.org, July 1. http://blog.norml .org/2014/07/01/heres-what-colorado-looks-like-6-months-into-legalization/.

Ferris, Kerry, and Jill Stein. 2016. *The Real World: An Introduction to Sociology*. 5th ed. New York: Norton.

Festinger, Leon, Henry W. Riecken, and Stanley Schachter. 1956. *When Prophecy Fails: A Social and Psychological Study of a Modern Group That Predicted the Destruction of the World*. Minneapolis: University of Minnesota Press.

Fine, Gary Alan. 2001. *Difficult Reputations: Collective Memories of the Evil, Inept, and Controversial*. Chicago: University of Chicago Press.

———. 2007. *Authors of the Storm: Meteorologists and the Culture of Prediction*. Chicago: University of Chicago Press.

———. 2012. *Sticky Reputations: The Politics of Collective Memory in Mid-century America*. New York: Routledge.

Fischer, David Hackett. 1970. *Historians' Fallacies: Toward a Logic of Historical Thought*. New York: Harper and Row.

Flaherty, Colleen. 2016. "Confronting the Past." *Inside Higher Ed,* January8.www.insidehighered.com/news/2016/01/08/historians-debate-value-and-place-confederate-monuments-and-other-symbols.

Flanagin, Jake. 2014. "The Tragedy of America's Dog: A Brief History of the Vilification of the Pit Bull." *Pacific Standard,* February 28. www.psmag.com/nature-and-technology/tragedy-americas-dog-pit-bull-75642.

Forbes.com. 2015. "The Richest People in America." September 29. www.forbes.com/forbes-400.

Foundation for Traffic Safety. 2011. *Unlicensed to Kill.* Washington, DC: American Automobile Association. www.aaafoundation.org/sites/default/files/2011Unlicensed2Kill.pdf.

Fourcade, Marion. 2009. *Economists and Societies: Discipline and Profession in the United States, Britain, and France, 1980s to 1990s.* Princeton, NJ: Princeton University Press.

FOX News Insider. 2014. "Judge Nap: Obama Directly Caused Surge of Immigrant Children at Border." June 9. http://insider.foxnews.com/2014/06/09/judge-nap-obama-directly-caused-surge-illegal-immigrant-children-borders.

Fox, Steve, Paul Armentano, and Mason Tvert. 2009. *Marijuana Is Safer: So Why Are We Driving People to Drink?* White River Junction, VT: Chelsea Green.

Freidson, Eliot. 1986. *Professional Powers: A Study of the Institutionalization of Formal Knowledge.* Chicago: University of Chicago Press.

Friedman, Lee S., Donald Hedeker, and Elihu D. Richter. 2009. "Long-Term Effects of Repealing the National Maximum Speed Limit in the United States." *American Journal of Public Health* 99: 1626–31.

Furedi, Frank. 1997. *Culture of Fear: Risk-Taking and the Morality of Low Expectation.* London: Cassell.

———. 2009. "What Swine Flu Reveals about the Culture of Fear: A Guide to Today's Various Species of Scaremonger." *Spiked.com,* May 5. www.spiked-online.com/newsite/article/6633#.V2fxi6Ifosk.

———. 2012. "The Savile Inquiries: Giving Truth a Bad Name." *Spiked.com,* October 24. www.spiked-online.com/newsite/article/13012#.V2fwXqIfosl.

———. 2013a. *Moral Crusades in an Age of Mistrust: The Jimmy Savile Scandal.* New York: Palgrave Macmillan.

———. 2013b. "Why South London's 'Slave' House Is Nothing of the Sort." *Guardian.com,* November 26. www.theguardian .com/commentisfree/2013/nov/26/south-london-slave-house-slavery-hysteria.

———. 2015. "No, It's Not 'Just Like Slavery': So-Called Modern Slavery Is More Fiction Than Fact." *Spiked.com,* August 3. www.spiked-online.com/newsite/article/no-its-not-just-like-slavery/17254#. V2ory6Ifosk.

———. 2016. "The Cultural Underpinning of Concept Creep." *Psychological Inquiry* 27:34–39.

Furner, Mary O. 1975. *Advocacy and Objectivity: A Crisis in the Professionalization of American Social Science, 1865–1905.* Lexington: University Press of Kentucky.

Galbraith, John Kenneth. 1990. *A Short History of Financial Euphoria.* New York: Penguin.

Gallup Poll. 2015. "Trends A to Z: Abortion." www.gallup.com/poll /1576/Abortion.aspx.

Gans, Herbert J. 1997. "Best-Sellers by Sociologists: An Exploratory Study." *Contemporary Sociology* 26:131–35.

Ganzeboom, Harry B.G., Donald J. Treiman, and Wout C. Ultee. 1991. "Comparative Intergenerational Stratification Research: Three Generations and Beyond." *Annual Review of Sociology* 17: 277–302.

Gattone, Charles F. 2006. *The Social Scientist as Public Intellectual: Critical Reflections in a Changing World.* Lanham, MD: Rowman and Littlefield.

———. 2012. "The Social Scientist as Public Intellectual in an Age of Mass Media." *International Journal of Politics, Culture, and Society* 25: 175–86.

Gettysburg National Military Park. 2015. "Statement Regarding the Confederate Flag." Press release. www.nps.gov/gett/learn/news /statement-regarding-the-confederate-flag.htm.

———. 2016. "Flags of the Civil War Centennial." National Park Service. Accessed May 10. www.nps.gov/media/photo/gallery.htm?id= C78A0AA0–155D-451F-6792278A97619590.

Gilbert, Michael A. 1996. *How to Win an Argument: Surefire Strategies for Getting Your Point Across.* 2nd ed. New York: MJF Books.

Giovagnoli, Mary. 2010. "Immigration Revelations Just the Tip of the ICEberg." *Alternet.org,* April 3. www.alternet.org/story/146294 /immigration_revelations_just_the_tip_of_the_iceberg.

Gladwell, Malcolm. 2000. *The Tipping Point: How Little Things Can Make a Big Difference.* Boston: Little, Brown.

———. 2008. *Outliers: The Story of Success.* Boston: Little, Brown.

Global @dvisor. 2012. *Mayan Prophecy: The End of the World?* IPSOS. April. www.ipsos-na.com/download/pr.aspx?id=11706.

Goetze, Rolf. 1983. *Rescuing the American Dream: Public Policies and the Crisis in Housing.* New York: Holmes and Meier.

Gold, Alex, Edward Rodrigue, and Richard V. Reeves. 2015. "Following the Success Sequence? Success Is More Likely If You're White." Brookings: Social Mobility Memos. August 6. www.brookings.edu /blogs/social-mobility-memos/posts/2015/08/06-following-success-sequence-race-reeves.

Gommo, Joni. 2015. "Are Smart Guns a Slippery Slope to Gun Control?" *Newsmax.com,* June 3. www.newsmax.com/FastFeatures/smart-guns-slippery-slope/2015/06/03/id/648427/.

Goodman, Ellen. 1989. "Babies Born Addicted: Off to a Bad Start." *St. Louis Post-Dispatch,* August 21.

Gordon, Liahna E. 2013. "Wankers, Inverts, and Addicts: The Scientific Construction of Asexuality as a Social Problem." In *Making Sense of Social Problems: New Images, New Issues,* edited by Joel Best and Scott R. Harris, 111–33. Boulder, CO: Lynne Rienner.

Gormley, William T. 2012. *Voices for Children: Rhetoric and Public Policy.* Washington, DC: Brookings Institution Press.

Greenfield, Kent. 2013. "The Slippery Slope to Polygamy and Incest." *American Prospect.org,* July 15. http://prospect.org/article/slippery-slope-polygamy-and-incest.

Gross, Neil, and Solon Simmons. 2014. "The Social and Political Views of American College and University Professors." In *Professors and Their Politics,* edited by Neil Gross and Solon Simmons, 19–49. Baltimore, MD: Johns Hopkins University Press.

Grundmann, Reiner. 2011. "'Climategate' and the Scientific Ethos." *Science, Technology, and Human Values* 38: 67–93.

Gusfield, Joseph R. 1993. "The Social Symbolism of Smoking and Health." In *Smoking Policy: Law, Politics, and Culture,* edited by Robert L. Rabin and Stephen D. Sugarman, 49–68. New York: Oxford University Press.

Hagelin, Rebecca. 2012. "Abortion's Slippery Slope: When People Aren't 'Persons.'" *Townhall.com,* March 14. http://townhall.com/columnists /rebeccahagelin/2012/03/14/abortions_slippery_slope_when_people_ arent_persons.

Halzack, Sarah. 2015. "Toying with Changes in Gender Marketing." *Washington Post,* December 5.

Hamilton, Richard F., and Lowell L. Hargens. 1993. "The Politics of the Professors: Self-Identification, 1969–1984." *Social Forces* 71: 603–27.

Hannity and Colmes. 2004. "Interview with James Dobson." *FOX News,* May 17.

Hanson, Sandra L., and John Zogby. 2010. "Trends—Attitudes about the American Dream." *Public Opinion Quarterly* 74: 570–84.

Harford, Tim. 2006. *The Undercover Economist: Exposing Why the Rich Are Rich, the Poor Are Poor—and Why You Can Never Buy a Decent Used Car!* New York: Oxford University Press.

———. 2014. *The Undercover Economist Strikes Back: How to Run—or Ruin—an Economy.* New York: Riverhead Books.

Harris, Richard. 1976. "A Reporter at Large: Handguns." *New Yorker,* July 26: 53–58.

Haskins, Ron. 2013. "Your Future Is Your Choice." *Washington Post,* March 13.

Haun, Marjorie. 2015. "The Unexpected Side Effects of Legalizing Weed." *Newsweek.com,* June 6. www.newsweek.com/unexpected-side-effects-legalizing-weed-339931.

Hellerstein, Erica, and Judd Legum. 2016. "The Phony Debate about Political Correctness." *Thinkprogress.org,* January 14. http://think-progress.org/politics/2016/01/14/3737907/the-phony-debate-about-political-correctness/.

Henigan, Dennis A. 2016. *"Guns Don't Kill People, People Kill People": And Other Myths about Guns and Gun Control.* Boston: Beacon.

Henslin, James M. 2014. *Sociology: A Down-to-Earth Approach*. 12th ed. Upper Saddle River, NJ: Pearson.

Hertz, Rosanna. 2010. "Economic Crisis and New Social Realities: Bait and Switch and the American Dream." *Sociological Forum* 25: 643–54.

Hilgartner, Stephen, and Charles L. Bosk. 1988. "The Rise and Fall of Social Problems." *American Journal of Sociology* 94: 53–78.

Hogenboom, Melissa. 2012. "A Tipping Point in the Fight against Slavery?" *BBC Magazine,* October 19.

Hogue, Ilyse. 2014. "Statement: NARAL Pro-Choice America Reaction to the Supreme Court Decision on Hobby Lobby." *NARAL Pro-Choice American.org,* June 30. www.prochoiceamerica.org/media /press-releases/2014/pr06302014_scotus_hobbylobby.html.

Holmes, Robert, and M. Christine Cagle. 2000. "The Great Debate: White Support for and Black Opposition to the Confederate Battle Flag." In *Confederate Symbols in the Contemporary South,* edited by J. Michael Martinez, William D. Richardson, and Ron McNinch-Su, 281–302. Gainesville: University Press of Florida.

Holyfield, Lori, Matthew Ryan Moltz, and Mindy S. Bradley. 2009. "Race Discourse and the U.S. Confederate Flag." *Race, Ethnicity and Education* 12: 517–37.

Howe, Neil. 2014. *Generations in Pursuit of the American Dream*. Saeculum Research. www.lifecourse.com/assets/files/reports/Generations% 20in%20Pursuit%20of%20the%20American%20Dream.pdf.

Hughes, Michael, and Carolyn J. Kroehler. 2008. *Sociology: The Core*. 8th ed. New York: McGraw-Hill.

Hui, Sylvia. 2012. "Britain Bedeviled by Binge Drinking." *Washington Post,* May 22.

Hutchings, Vincent L., Hanes Walton Jr., and Andrea Benjamin. 2010. "The Impact of Explicit Racial Cues on Gender Differences in Support for Confederate Symbols and Partisanship." *Journal of Politics* 72: 1175–88.

Hynes, Patricia. 2015. "No 'Magic Bullets': Children, Young People, Trafficking, and Child Protection in the UK." *International Migration* 53 (4): 62–76. www.bbc.com/news/magazine-19831913.

Igo, Sarah E. 2007. *The Averaged American: Surveys, Citizens, and the Making of a Mass Public*. Cambridge, MA: Harvard University Press.

Ingraham, Christopher. 2015. "People Are Getting Shot by Toddlers on a Weekly Basis This Year." *Washington Post Wonkblog*, October 14. www.washingtonpost.com/news/wonk/wp/2015/10/14/people-are-getting-shot-by-toddlers-on-a-weekly-basis-this-year/.

Isaacs, Julia B. 2008. "International Comparisons of Economic Mobility." In *Getting Ahead or Losing Ground: Economic Mobility in America,* by Isabel V. Sawhill, Julia B. Isaacs, and Ron Haskins, chap. 3. New York: Pew Charitable Trusts Economic Mobility Project. www.brookings.edu/~/media/research/files/reports/2008/2/economic-mobility-sawhill/02_economic_mobility_sawhill_ch3.pdf.

Jacobs, James B. 2002. *Can Gun Control Work?* New York: Oxford University Press.

Jacobs, Ronald N., and Eleanor Townsley. 2011. *The Space of Opinion: Media Intellectuals and the Public Sphere.* New York: Oxford University Press.

Jaschik, Scott. 2015. "Vandalism or Protest?" *Inside Higher Ed,* July 8. www.insidehighered.com/news/2015/07/08/what-should-educators-make-spray-painting-campus-statues-and-symbols-old-south.

———. 2016a. "Princeton Keeps Wilson Name." *Inside Higher Ed,* April 5. www.insidehighered.com/news/2016/04/05/princeton-will-keep-woodrow-wilson-name.

———. 2016b. "Yale Retains Calhoun Name." *Inside Higher Ed,* April 28. www.insidehighered.com/news/2016/04/28/yale-will-keep-calhoun-name-residential-college-and-drop-use-term-master.

Jenkins, John Major. 2009. *The 2012 Story: The Myths, Fallacies, and Truth behind the Most Intriguing Date in History.* New York: Tarcher.

Jenkins, Philip. 1998. *Moral Panic: Changing Concepts of the Child Molester in Modern America.* New Haven, CT: Yale University Press.

Jhally, Sut, and Justin Lewis. 1992. *Enlightened Racism: The Cosby Show, Audiences, and the Myth of the American Dream.* Boulder, CO: Westview.

Jones, Jeffrey M. 2015. "Democrats' Views on Confederate Flag Increasingly Negative." *Gallup.com,* July 8. www.gallup.com/poll/184040/democrats-views-confederate-flag-increasingly-negative.aspx.

Jones, Julia, and Eve Bower. 2015. "American Death in Terrorism vs. Gun Violence in One Graph." *CNN.com,* December 30. www.cnn.com/2015/10/02/us/oregon-shooting-terrorism-gun-violence/.

Joseph, Lawrence E. 2007. *Apocalypse 2012: An Optimist Investigates the End of Civilization*. London: HarperElement.

Kalleberg, Ragnvald. 2012. "Sociologists as Public Intellectuals and Experts." *Journal of Applied Social Science* 6: 3–52.

Kaplan, John. 1970. *Marijuana: The New Prohibition*. New York: World.

Kennedy, Edward M. 2008. "How to Fix 'No Child.'" *Washington Post*, January 7.

King, David. 1997. *The Commissar Vanishes: The Falsification of Photographs and Art in Stalin's Russia*. New York: Metropolitan Books.

Kinney, Martha E. 1998. "'If Vanquished I Am Still Victorious': Religious and Cultural Symbolism in Virginia's Confederate Memorial Day Celebrations, 1866–1930." *Virginia Magazine of History and Biography* 106: 237–66.

Klein, Daniel B., and Carlotta Stern. 2005. "Political Diversity in Six Disciplines." *Academic Questions* 18: 40–52.

Kowalchuk, Lisa, and Neil McLaughlin. 2009. "Mapping the Social Space of Opinion: Public Sociology and the Op-Ed in Canada." *Canadian Journal of Sociology* 34: 697–728.

Kubal, Timothy. 2008. *Cultural Movements and Collective Memory: Christopher Columbus and the Rewriting of the National Origin Myth*. New York: Palgrave Macmillan.

Kytle, Ethan J., and Blain Roberts. 2015. "Take Down the Confederate Flags, but Not the Monuments." *Atlantic.com*, June 25. www.theatlantic.com/politics/archive/2015/06/-confederate-monuments-flags-south-carolina/396836/.

Ladd, Everett Carll, Jr., and Seymour Martin Lipset. 1975. *The Divided Academy: Professors and Politics*. New York: McGraw-Hill.

Lakoff, George, and Mark Johnson. 2003. *Metaphors We Live By*. Chicago: University of Chicago Press.

LaPierre, W. 1994. *Guns, Crime, and Freedom*. New York: Regnery.

Lawrence, Robert Z. 2016. "Does Productivity Still Determine Worker Compensation? Domestic and International Evidence." In *The U.S. Labor Market: Questions and Challenges for Public Policy*, edited by Michael R. Strain, 42–61. Washington, DC: American Enterprise Institute.

Lebaron, Frèdèric. 2006. "'Nobel' Economists as Public Intellectuals: The Circulation of Symbolic Capital." *International Journal of Contemporary Sociology* 43 (1): 88–101.

Lee, M.J. 2015. "Walmart, Amazon, Sears, eBay to Stop Selling Confederate Flag Merchandise." *CNN.com*, June 24. www.cnn.com/2015/06/22/politics/confederate-flag-walmart-south-carolina/.

Leon, Carol Boyd. 2016. "The Life of American Workers in 1915." *Monthly Labor Review*, February. www.bls.gov/opub/mlr/2016/article/the-life-of-american-workers-in-1915.htm.

Levitt, Sasha. 2016. Personal communication.

Levitt, Steven D., and Stephen J. Dubner. 2005. *Freakonomics: A Rogue Economist Explores the Hidden Side of Everything*. New York: Morrow.

———. 2009. *SuperFreakonomics: Global Cooling, Patriotic Prostitutes, and Why Suicide Bombers Should Buy Life Insurance*. New York: Morrow.

———. 2014. *Think Like a Freak: The Authors of Freakonomics Offer to Retrain Your Brain*. New York: Morrow.

Lewis, Michael. 2016. *The Undoing Project: A Friendship That Changed Our Minds*. New York: Norton.

Lin, Kai. 2017. "The Medicalization and Demedicalization of Kink: Shifting Contexts of Sexual Politics." *Sexualities* 20: 302–23.

Lipset, Seymour Martin, and Reinhard Bendix. 1959. *Social Mobility in Industrial Society*. Berkeley: University of California Press.

Lithwick, Dahlia. 2013. "Conscience Creep: What's So Wrong with Conscience Clauses?" *Slate.com*, October 3. www.slate.com/articles/news_and_politics/jurisprudence/2013/10/is_there_a_principled_way_to_respond_to_the_proliferation_of_conscience.html.

Longhofer, Wesley, Shannon Golden, and Arturo Baiocchi. 2010. "A Fresh Look at Sociology Bestsellers." *Contexts* 9 (May): 18–25.

Loseke, Donileen R. 2003. *Thinking about Social Problems*. 2nd ed. Hawthorne, NY: Aldine de Gruyter.

Lukianoff, Greg, and Jonathan Haidt. 2015. "The Coddling of the American Mind." *Atlantic*. September. www.theatlantic.com/magazine/archive/2015/09/the-coddling-of-the-american-mind/399356/.

Macionis, John J. 2009. *Society: The Basics*, 10th ed. Upper Saddle River, NJ: Pearson.

Maier, Mark H., and Jennifer Imazeki. 2012. *The Data Game: Controversies in Social Science Statistics.* 4th ed. New York: Routledge.

Marchant, Gary. 2015. "A.I. Thee Wed: Humans Should Be Able to Marry Robots." *Slate.com,* August 10. www.slate.com/articles/technology /future_tense/2015/08/humans_should_be_able_to_marry_robots .single.html.

Martin, Alyson, and Nushin Rashidian. 2014. *A New Leaf: The End of Cannabis Prohibition.* New York: New Press.

Martin, Kevin P. 2015. "Drug Abuse Is Not a Victimless Crime." *New Boston Post,* November 3. http://newbostonpost.com/2015/11/03 /drug-abuse-is-not-a-victimless-crime/.

Martinez, J. Michael. 2008. "The Georgia Confederate Flag Dispute." *Georgia Historical Quarterly* 92: 200–228.

Martinez, J. Michael, and Robert M. Harris. 2000. "Graves, Works, and Epitaphs: Confederate Monuments in the Southern Landscape." In *Confederate Symbols in the Contemporary South,* edited by J. Michael Martinez, William D. Richardson, and Ron McNinch-Su, 130–92. Gainesville: University Press of Florida.

Mathis-Lilley, Ben. 2015. "Rep. Steve King Says Obergefell Ruling Means You Can Marry a Lawnmower." *Slate.com,* July 30. www .slate.com/blogs/the_slatest/2015/07/30/steve_king_marrying_ a_lawnmower_iowa_congressman_imagines_strange_desires.html.

Mattera, Joseph. 2015. "With Sexbots Gaining Momentum, Are Human-Robot Marriages Inevitable?" *Charisma News.com,* May 14. www.charismanews.com/opinion/the-pulse/49628-with-sexbots-gaining-momentum-are-human-robot-marriages-inevitable.

Mattson, Margaret E., Earl S. Pollack, and Joseph W. Cullen. 1987. "What Are the Odds That Smoking Will Kill You?" *American Journal of Public Health* 77: 425–31.

McCright, Aaron M., and Riley E. Dunlap. 2000. "Challenging Global Warming as a Social Problem: An Analysis of the Conservative Movement's Counter-Claims." *Social Problems* 47: 499–522.

———. 2003. "Defeating Kyoto: The Conservative Movement's Impact on U.S. Climate Change Policy." *Social Problems* 50: 348–73.

———. 2011. "The Politicization of Climate Change and Polarization in the American Public's Views of Global Warming, 2001–2010." *Sociological Quarterly* 52: 155–94.

McFadden, Robert D. 2013. "Harold Camping, Dogged Forecaster of the End of the World, Dies at 92." *New York Times,* December 18.

McGirr, Lisa. 2016. *The War on Alcohol: Prohibition and the Rise of the American State.* New York: Norton.

McNinch-Su, Ron, William D. Richardson, and J. Michael Martinez. 2000. "Traditionalists versus Reconstructionists: The Case of the Georgia State Flag, Part One." In *Confederate Symbols in the Contemporary South,* edited by J. Michael Martinez, William D. Richardson, and Ron McNinch-Su, 303–21. Gainesville: University Press of Florida.

McRaney, David. 2013. *You Are Now Less Dumb: How to Conquer Mob Mentality, How to Buy Happiness, and All the Other Ways to Outsmart Yourself.* New York: Gotham.

Meacham, John 2012. "Keeping the Dream Alive." *Time* (July 2): 26–29, 32–33, 35, 39.

Merton, Robert K. 1938. "Social Structure and Anomie." *American Sociological Review* 3: 672–82.

Miles, Rufus E. 1976. *Awakening from the American Dream: The Social and Political Limits to Growth.* New York: Universe.

Miller. Geoffrey. 2009. *Spent: Sex, Evolution, and Consumer Behavior.* New York: Viking.

Miracle, Jaime. 2015. "Testimony to the Ohio Senate Health and Human Services Committee Opposing Senate Bill 127." Ohio Legislative Information Systems, June 24. search-prod.lis.state.oh.us/ … /sb127jaimemiracleopp.pdf.

Mirowski, Philip. 2010. "The Great Mortification: Economists' Responses to the Crisis of 2007–(and Counting)." *Hedgehog Review* 12 (Summer): 28–41.

Mochnacki, Alex, Aaron Segaert, and Neil McLaughlin. 2009. "Public Sociology in Print: A Comparative Analysis of Book Publishing in Three Social Science Disciplines." *Canadian Journal of Sociology* 34: 729–64.

Mohun, Arwen P. 2013. *Risk: Negotiating Safety in American Society.* Baltimore, MD: Johns Hopkins University Press.

Mora, Edwin. 2015. "Sen. Ted Cruz: American Dream and U.S. Leadership in the World Are Slipping Away." *Breitbart.com*, January 18. www.breitbart.com/big-government/2015/01/18/sen-ted-cruz-american-dream-and-u-s-leadership-in-the-world-are-slipping-away/.

Morello, Lauren. 2012. "Is Earth Nearing an Environmental 'Tipping Point'?" *Scientific American.com*, June 7. www.scientificamerican.com/article/is-earth-nearing-environmental-tipping-point/.

Morris, C. Craig. 2009. *Motorcycle Trends in the United States.* Bureau of Transportation Statistics. May. www.rita.dot.gov/bts/sites/rita.dot.gov.bts/files/publications/special_reports_and_issue_briefs/special_report/2009_05_14/pdf/entire.pdf.

Morrison, David. 2009. "2012 and Counting: A NASA Scientist Answers the Top 20 Questions about 2012." *Skeptic* 15 (20): 47–53.

Moseley, William G., and Dillon Teske. 2011. "Geographers in the Public Square: A Comparative Analysis of Op-Ed Productivity." *Applied Geography* 31: 232–36.

Mosier, Jeff. 2015. "Six Flags Over Texas Started Distancing from the Confederate Battle Flag Decades Ago." *Scoop Blog, Dallas Morning News*, June 29. http://thescoopblog.dallasnews.com/2015/06/six-flags-over-texas-started-distancing-from-the-confederate-battle-flag-decades-ago.html/.

Motel, Seth. 2015. "6 Facts about Marijuana." Pew Research Center. April 14. www.pewresearch.org/fact-tank/2015/04/14/6-facts-about-marijuana/.

Mothers Against Drunk Driving. 2013. "New Data on Teen Emergency Room Visits." June 13. www.madd.org/blog/2013/june/new-data-on-teen-emergency.html.

Muggeridge, Tessa. 2011. "Republican Lawmaker: Ban Abortions Sought Because of Race or Sex." *Arizona Capitol Times.com*, February 2. http://azcapitoltimes.com/news/2011/02/02/republican-lawmaker-ban-abortions-sought-because-of-race-or-sex/#ixzz4Bf5Mbl9d.

Munch, Glenn R. 1999. *About Y2K: The Survival Guide and Handbook of Practical Preparations.* Baltimore: Genmet.

Murray, Charles A. 2012a. *Coming Apart: The State of White America, 1960–2010.* New York: Crown.

———. 2012b. "The 3 Laws of Social Programs." *AEIdeas* (American Enterprise Institute), December 10. www.aei.org/publication/the-3-laws-of-social-programs/.

National Center for Children in Poverty. 2104. "Child Poverty." www.nccp.org/topics/childpoverty.html.

National Center for Statistics and Analysis. 2014. *2013 Motor Vehicle Crashes: Overview.* Traffic Safety Facts Research Note. Report No. DOT HS 812 101. Washington, DC: National Highway Traffic Safety Administration.

———. 2015. *Children: 2013 Data.* Traffic Safety Facts, Report No. DOT HS 812 154. Washington, DC: National Highway Traffic Safety Administration.

National Highway Traffic Safety Administration. 2013. *Traffic Safety Facts 2012.* Washington, DC: National Highway Traffic Safety Administration. www-nrd.nhtsa.dot.gov/Pubs/812032.pdf.

National Institute on Alcohol Abuse and Alcoholism. 2015. "Alcohol Facts and Statistics." www.niaaa.nih.gov/alcohol-health/overview-alcohol-consumption/alcohol-facts-and-statistics.

National Opinion Research Center. 1999. *Gambling Impact and Behavior Study.* April 1. www.norc.org/PDFs/publications/GIBSFinalReportApril1999.pdf.

Neff, John R. 2005. *Honoring the Civil War Dead: Commemoration and the Problem of Reconciliation.* Lawrence: University Press of Kansas.

Newman, David M. 2000. *Sociology: Exploring the Architecture of Everyday Life.* 3rd ed. Thousand Oaks, CA: Sage.

———. 2017. *Sociology: Exploring the Architecture of Everyday Life.* 11th ed. Thousand Oaks, CA: Sage.

Newman, Joshua I. 2007. "Old Times There Are Not Forgotten: Sport, Identity, and the Confederate Flag in the Dixie South." *Sociology of Sport Journal* 24: 261–82.

Newman, Katherine S. 1993. *Declining Fortunes: The Withering of the American Dream.* New York: Basic Books.

Newport, Frank. 2015. "Many Americans Doubt They Will Get Social Security Benefits." *Gallup.com,* August 13. www.gallup.com/poll/184580/americans-doubt-social-security-benefits.aspx.

Obama, Barack. 2014. "Message to Congress Transmitting the Economic Report of the President." *American Presidency Project,* March 10. www.presidency.ucsb.edu/ws/?pid=104792.

———. 2015. "Remarks on the Shootings in Roseburg, Oregon." *American Presidency Project,* October 1. www.presidency.ucsb.edu/ws/index.php?pid=110922&st=&st1=.

———. 2016. "Remarks on Gun Violence." *American Presidency Project,* January 5. www.presidency.ucsb.edu/ws/index.php?pid=111391&st=slippery+slope&st1=.

Office of Highway Policy Information. 2012. "Our Nation's Highways: 2011." Federal Highway Administration. www.fhwa.dot.gov/policyinformation/pubs/hf/pl11028/chapter4.cfm.

Oreskes, Naomi, and Erik M. Conway. 2010. *Merchants of Doubt: How a Handful of Scientists Obscured the Truth on Issues from Tobacco Smoke to Global Warming.* New York: Bloomsbury.

Parnass, Sarah. 2013. "Republicans Predict Fraud, Bestiality If Gay Marriage Is Legalized." *ABC News,* April 4. http://abcnews.go.com/blogs/politics/2013/04/republicans-predict-fraud-bestiality-if-gay-marriage-is-legalized/.

Peters, Jeremy W. 2016. "Marco Rubio Takes Darker Tone, Saying American Dream 'Is Dying.'" First Draft. *New York Times,* January 11. www.nytimes.com/politics/first-draft/2016/01/11/marco-rubio-takes-darker-tone-saying-american-dream-is-dying/.

Pew Charitable Trusts Economic Mobility Project. 2012. *Pursuing the American Dream: Economic Mobility across Generations.* Washington, DC: Pew Charitable Trusts. www.pewtrusts.org/~/media/legacy/uploadedfiles/pcs_assets/2012/pursuingamericandreampdf.pdf.

Pew Research Center. 2013. *Majority Now Supports Legalizing Marijuana.* April 4. www.people-press.org/2013/04/04/majority-now-supports-legalizing-marijuana/.

———. 2014. "Growing Public Support for Gun Rights." December 10. www.people-press.org/2014/12/10/growing-public-support-for-gun-rights/.

Pfeffer, Fabian T., and Florian R. Hertel. 2015. "How Has Educational Expansion Shaped Social Mobility Trends in the United States?" *Social Forces* 94: 143–80.

Pfohl, Stephen J. 1977. "The 'Discovery' of Child Abuse." *Social Problems* 24: 310–23.

Poe, Richard. 2001. *The Seven Myths of Gun Control: Reclaiming the Truth about Guns, Crime, and the Second Amendment.* New York: Three Rivers.

Polygamy.com. 2015. "Polyamorous Rights Advocates See Marriage Equality Coming for Them." October 15. www.polygamy.com /articles/22739026/polyamorous-rights-advocates-see-marriage-equality-coming-for-them.

Posner, Richard A. 2001. *Public Intellectuals: A Study of Decline.* Cambridge, MA: Harvard University Press.

Prince, K. Michael. 2004. *Rally 'Round the Flag, Boys! South Carolina and the Confederate Flag.* Columbia: University of South Carolina Press.

Public Policy Polling. 2015. "National Survey Results." Gun Owners Poll. November 11–12. https://cdn.americanprogress.org/wp-content/uploads/2015/11/17054452/PPP-GunOwnersPollResults-11.17.15 .pdf.

Putnam, Robert D. 2015. *Our Kids: The American Dream in Crisis.* New York: Simon and Schuster.

Qui, Linda. 2015. "Fact-Checking a Comparison of Gun Deaths and Terrorism Deaths." *PolitiFact.com,* October 5. www.politifact.com /truth-o-meter/statements/2015/oct/05/viral-image/fact-checking-comparison-gun-deaths-and-terrorism-/.

Quigley, Kevin F. 2005. "Bug Reactions: Considering US Government and UK Government Y2K Operations in Light of Media Coverage and Public Opinion Polls." *Health, Risk and Society* 7:267–91.

Rank, Mark Robert, Thomas A. Hirschl, and Kirk A. Foster. 2014. *Chasing the American Dream: Understanding What Shapes Our Fortunes.* New York: Oxford University Press.

Rector, Robert, and Rachel Sheffield. 2011. *Air Conditioning, Cable TV, and an Xbox: What Is Poverty in the United States Today?* Heritage Foundation Backgrounder 2517. July 19. www.heritage.org/Research /Reports/2011/07/What-is-Poverty.

Reeves, Richard V. 2014a. "Is America Dreaming?: Understanding Social Mobility." Brookings Institution. August 19. www.youtube.com /watch?v=t2XFh_tD2RA.

————. 2014b. "Saving Horatio Alger: Equality, Opportunity, and the American Dream." Brookings Institution. August 14. www.brookings .edu/research/essays/2014/saving-horatio-alger#.

Reeves, Richard V., and Nathan Joo. 2016. "How Much Social Mobility Do People Really Want?" Brookings Institution. January 12. www .brookings.edu/blog/social-mobility-memos/2016/01/12/how-much-social-mobility-do-people-really-want/.

Regnerus, Mark, David Gordon, and Joseph Price. 2016. "Documenting Pornography Use in America: A Comparative Analysis of Methodological Approaches." *Journal of Sex Research*. DOI: 10.1080 /00224499.2015.1096886.

Research Institute on Addictions. 2012. "RIA Reaching Others with Gambling Research." University at Buffalo, State University of New York. Spring. www.buffalo.edu/content/dam/www/ria/ES /ES3Gambling.pdf.

Restall, Matthew, and Amara Solari. 2011. *2012 and the End of the World: The Western Roots of the Maya Apocalypse.* Lanham, MD: Rowman and Littlefield.

Rinzler, Alan. 2010. "Shelf Wars: What Authors Need to Know about Bookstore Visibility." *The Book Deal,* April 13. http://alanrinzler .com/2010/04/shelf-wars-what-authors-need-to-know-about-bookstore-visibility/.

Ritzer, George. 2006. "Who's a Public Intellectual?" *British Journal of Sociology* 57: 209–13.

Roosevelt, Franklin D. 1937. "Message to Congress on Farm Tenancy." *American Presidency Project.* February 6. www.presidency.ucsb.edu /ws/?pid=15362.

Ropers, Richard H. 1991. *Persistent Poverty: The American Dream Turned Nightmare.* New York: Plenum.

Rovi, Sue, Ping-Hsin Chen, Marielos Vega, Mark S. Johnson, and Charles P. Mouton. 2009. "Mapping the Elder Mistreatment Iceberg: U.S. Hospitalizations with Elder Abuse and Neglect Diagnoses." *Journal of Elder Abuse and Neglect* 21:346–59.

Rudé, George F.E. 1964. *The Crowd in History: A Study of Popular Disturbances in France and England, 1730–1848.* New York: Wiley.

Saad, Lydia. 2011. "Self-Reported Gun Ownership in U.S. Is Highest Since 1993." *Gallup.com*, October 26. www.gallup.com/poll/150353 /Self-Reported-Gun-Ownership-Highest-1993.aspx.

Sabet, Kevin A. 2013. *Reefer Sanity: Seven Great Truths about Marijuana.* New York: Beaufort.

Saguy, Abigail C. 2003. *What Is Sexual Harassment? From Capitol Hill to the Sorbonne.* Berkeley: University of California Press.

Samuel, Lawrence R. 2012. *The American Dream: A Cultural History.* Syracuse, NY: Syracuse University Press.

Sanders, Bernie. 2015. "Public College Should Be Free." *Chicago Tribune*, October 23. www.chicagotribune.com/news/nationworld/ct-bernie-sanders-free-college-20151023-story.html.

Santow, Leonard J., and Mark E. Santow. 2005. *Social Security and the Middle-Class Squeeze: Fact and Fiction about America's Entitlement Programs.* Westport, CT: Praeger.

Scherer, Michael. 2013. "The NRA's Slippery Slope Strategy to Fight Background Checks." *Time.com*, April 11. http://swampland .time.com/2013/04/11/the-national-rifle-associations-slippery-slope-strategy/.

Schieber, Sylvester J., and John B. Shoven. 1999. *The Real Deal: The History and Future of Social Security.* New Haven, CT: Yale University Press.

Schudson, Michael. 1992. *Watergate in American Memory: How We Remember, Forget, and Reconstruct the Past.* New York: Basic Books.

Schuh, Scott, and Joanna Stavins. 2014. *The 2011 and 2012 Surveys of Consumer Payment Choice.* Federal Reserve Bank of Boston Research Data Reports no. 14–1. www.bostonfed.org/economic/rdr/2014 /rdr1401.pdf.

Schuman, Howard, Barry Schwartz, and Hannah D'Arcy. 2005. "Elite Revisionists and Popular Beliefs: Christopher Columbus, Hero or Villain?" *Public Opinion Quarterly* 69: 2–29.

Schur, Edwin M. 1965. *Crimes without Victims: Deviant Behavior and Pubic Policy.* Englewood Cliffs, NJ: Prentice-Hall.

Schwartz, Barry. 1987. *George Washington: The Making of an American Symbol.* New York: Free Press.

———. 2000. *Abraham Lincoln and the Forge of National Memory.* Chicago: University of Chicago Press.

———. 2008. *Abraham Lincoln in the Post-heroic Era*. Chicago: University of Chicago Press.

Schwarz, John E. 1997. *Illusions of Opportunity: The American Dream in Question*. New York: Norton.

Sheff, Elisabeth. 2011. "Polyamorous Families, Same-Sex Marriage, and the Slippery Slope." *Journal of Contemporary Ethnography* 40: 487–520.

Shpigel, Ben. 2012. "Football Faces 'Turning Point' on the Risk of Injuries." *New York Times,* June 21.

Sieber, Sam D. 2005. *Second-Rate Nation: From the American Dream to the American Myth*. Boulder, CO: Paradigm.

Simko, Christina. 2015. *The Politics of Consolation: Memory and the Meaning of September 11*. New York: Oxford University Press.

Slovic, Paul, ed. 2000. *The Perception of Risk*. New York: Earthscan.

———. 2010. *The Feeling of Risk: New Perspectives on Risk Perception*. New York: Earthscan.

Smith, R. Tyson, and Owen Whooley. 2015. "Dropping the Disorder in PTSD." *Contexts* 14 (Fall): 38–43.

Smith, Tom, and Jaesok Son. 2013. "Trends in Public Attitudes toward Abortion." *General Social Survey 2012 Final Report*. National Opinion Research Center. May. www.norc.org/PDFs/GSS%20Reports/Trends%20in%20Attitudes%20About%20Abortion_Final.pdf.

Solow, Robert M. 1985. "An Aversion to Saying 'I Don't Know': Why People Make Fun of Economists." *New York Times,* December 29.

Southern Poverty Law Center. 2016. *Whose Heritage? Public Symbols of the Confederacy*. April 21. www.splcenter.org/sites/default/files/whose heritage_splc.pdf.

Soyer, Michaela. 2016. *A Dream Denied: Incarceration, Recidivism, and Young Minority Men in America*. Berkeley: University of California Press.

Spaulding, Charles B., and Henry A. Turner. 1968. "Political Orientation and Field of Specialization among College Professors." *Sociology of Education* 41: 247–62.

Spector, Malcolm, and John I. Kitsuse. 1977. *Constructing Social Problems*. Menlo Park, CA: Cummings.

Spring, Joel. 2015. *Economization of Education: Human Capital, Global Corporations, Skills-Based Schooling*. New York: Routledge.

Springhall, John. 1998. *Youth, Popular Culture and Moral Panics: Penny Gaffs to Gangsta-Rap, 1830–1996.* New York: St. Martin's.

Stacey, Judith, and Tey Meadow. 2009. "New Slants on the Slippery Slope: The Politics of Polygamy and Gay Family Rights in South Africa and the United States." *Politics and Society* 37: 167–202.

Stamper, Kory. 2017. *Word by Word: The Secret Life of Dictionaries.* New York: Pantheon.

Starks, Brian. 2003. "The New Economy and the American Dream: Examining the Effect of Work Conditions on Beliefs about Economic Opportunity." *Sociological Quarterly* 44: 205–25.

Starr, Paul. 1982. *The Social Transformation of American Medicine.* New York: Basic.

Stenvoll, Dag. 2008. "Slippery Slopes in Political Discourse." In *Political Language and Metaphor: Interpreting and Changing the Political World,* edited by Terrell Carver and Jernej Pikalo, 28–40. New York: Routledge.

Sternheimer, Karen. 2015. *Pop Culture Panics: How Moral Crusaders Construct Meanings of Deviance and Delinquency.* New York: Routledge.

Stewart, Julie. 2012. "Fiction over Facts: How Competing Narrative Forms Explain Policy in a New Immigration Destination." *Sociological Forum* 27: 591–616.

Stokes, Dillard. 1956. *Social Security: Fact and Fancy.* Chicago: Regnery.

Stout, Christopher Timothy, and Danvy Le. 2012. "Living the Dream: Barack Obama and Blacks' Changing Perceptions of the American Dream." *Social Science Quarterly* 93: 1338–59.

Stuart, David. 2011. *The Order of Days: The Maya World and the Truth about 2012.* New York: Harmony.

Sullivan, Andrew. 1997. "Dialog on Gay Marriage: 4." *Slate.com,* March 21. www.slate.com/articles/news_and_politics/dialogues/features/1997/gay_marriage/_5.html.

Swarns, Rachel L. 2016. "Georgetown Confronts Its Role in Nation's Slave Trade." *New York Times,* April 17.

Swift, Art. 2014. "Americans Rely Less on Credit Cards Than in Previous Years." *Gallup.com,* April 25. www.gallup.com/poll/168668/americans-rely-less-credit-cards-previous-years.aspx.

———. 2015. "Americans' Desire for Stricter Gun Laws Up Sharply." *Gallup.com,* October 19. www.gallup.com/poll/186236/americans-desire-stricter-gun-laws-sharply.aspx.

Taylor, Susannah, Lisa A. Burke, Kathleen Wheatley, and Joanie Sompayrac. 2011. "Effectively Facilitating Gender Transition in the Workplace." *Employee Responsibilities and Rights Journal* 23 (2): 101–16.

Thaler, Richard H. 2015. *Misbehaving: The Making of Behavioral Economics.* New York: Norton.

Thaler, Richard H., and Cass R. Sunstein. 2009. *Nudge: Improving Decisions about Health, Wealth, and Happiness.* Rev. ed. New York: Penguin.

Thernstrom, Stephan. 1964. *Poverty and Progress: Social Mobility in a Nineteenth Century City.* Cambridge, MA: Harvard University Press.

Thiel-Stern, Shayla. 2014. *From the Dance Hall to Facebook: Teen Girls, Mass Media, and Moral Panic in the United States, 1905–2010.* Amherst: University of Massachusetts Press.

Time. 1957. "Social Security: The System Is Running in the Red." (August 26): 57.

Topping, Nigel. 2016. "Renewable Energy Is at a Tipping Point—Let's Push it." *GreenBiz.com,* May 5. www.greenbiz.com/article/renewable-energy-tipping-point-lets-accelerate.

Townsley, Eleanor. 2006. "The Public Intellectual Trope in the United States." *American Sociologist* 37 (Fall): 39–66.

Truman, Jennifer L., and Lynn Langton. 2014. *Criminal Victimization, 2013.* NCJ 247648. Washington, DC: Bureau of Justice Statistics, September.

Trump, Donald. 2015. "Here's Donald Trump's Presidential Announcement Speech." *Time.com,* June 16. http://time.com/3923128/donald-trump-announcement-speech/.

Ungar, Sheldon. 1992. "The Rise and (Relative) Decline of Global Warming as a Social Problem." *Sociological Quarterly* 33: 483–501.

———. 1998. "Bringing the Issue Back In: Comparing the Marketability of the Ozone Hole and Global Warming." *Social Problems* 45: 510–27.

Vardi, Itai. 2014. "Quantifying Accidents: Cars, Statistics, and Unintended Consequences in the Construction of Social Problems over Time." *Qualitative Sociology* 37: 345–67.

Viscelli, Steve. 2016. *The Big Rig: Trucking and the Decline of the American Dream*. Berkeley: University of California Press.

Volokh, Eugene. 2002–3. "The Mechanisms of the Slippery Slope." *Harvard Law Review* 116: 1026–137.

Wagner-Pacifici, Robin, and Barry Schwartz. 1991. "The Vietnam Veterans Memorial: Commemorating a Difficult Past." *American Journal of Sociology* 97: 376–420.

Walton, Douglas. 1992. *Slippery Slope Arguments*. Oxford, U.K.: Clarendon Press.

Warner, Kee, and Harvey Molotch. 1993. "Information in the Marketplace: Media Explanations of the '87 Crash." *Social Problems* 40: 167–88.

Warner, W. Lloyd. (1949) 1960. *Social Class in America*. New York: Harper and Row.

Webroot.com. 2015. "Internet Pornography by the Numbers: A Significant Threat to Society." Accessed November 30. www.webroot.com/us/en/home/resources/tips/digital-family-life/internet-pornography-by-the-numbers.

Webster, Gerald R., and Jonathan I. Leib. 2001. "Whose South Is It Anyway? Race and the Confederate Battle Flag in South Carolina." *Political Geography* 20: 271–99.

———. 2002. "Political Culture, Religion, and the Confederate Battle Flag Debate in Alabama." *Journal of Political Geography* 20: 1–26.

Welch, Michael. 2000. *Flag Burning: Moral Panic and the Criminalization of Protest*. Hawthorne, NY: Aldine de Gruyter.

Wexler, Ellen. 2016. "Is the Word 'Plantation' Racist?" *Inside Higher Ed*, February 22. www.insidehighered.com/news/2016/02/22/cornell-plantations-focus-debate-language-slavery.

Whittaker, Julie M. 2015. "Alternative Inflation Measures for the Social Security Cost-of-Living Adjustment (COLA)." CRS Report R43363. Congressional Research Service. October 15. www.fas.org/sgp/crs/misc/R43363.pdf.

Wilcox, W. Bradford. 2016. "The Math Favors Married Parents." *AEIdeas* (American Enterprise Institute), March 22. www.aei.org/publication/the-math-favors-married-parents/?utm_source=paramount&utm_medium=email&utm_content=AEITHISWEEK&utm_campaign=Weekly032616.

Winkler, Adam. 2011. *Gunfight: The Battle over the Right to Bear Arms in America.* New York: Norton.

Winship, Scott. 2016. "Why Are Fewer Adults Surpassing Their Parents' Incomes?" Foundation for Research on Equal Opportunity. December 9. https://freopp.org/the-new-chetty-bomb-fewer-adults-are-surpassing-their-parents-income-3b7e6od93b24#.9wv7g3tdm.

Wolters, Justin. 2015. "How Economists Came to Dominate the Conversation." *Upshot,* January 23. www.nytimes.com/2015/01/24/upshot/how-economists-came-to-dominate-the-conversation.html.

Woods, Joshua. 2015. "The Op-Ed Sociologists: The Matthew Effect in Op-Ed Publication Patterns." *American Sociologist* 46: 356–72.

WorldNetDaily. 2016. "Violence 'Tip of Iceberg' of Porn's Destructive Influence."January17.www.wnd.com/2016/01/violence-tip-of-iceberg-of-porns-destructive-influence/#uAoeaRbtShk3pQ1b.99.

Wright, James D., Peter H. Rossi, and Kathleen Daly. 1983. *Under the Gun: Weapons, Crime, and Violence in America.* New York: Aldine.

Wuthnow, Robert. 1996. *Poor Richard's Principle: Recovering the American Dream through the Moral Dimension of Work, Business, and Money.* Princeton, NJ: Princeton University Press.

Young, Anna M. 2014. *Prophets, Gurus, and Pundits.* Carbondale: Southern Illinois University Press.

You've Earned a Say. 2015. "Updating Social Security for the 21st Century: 12 Proposals You Should Know About." *AARP.com,* October. www.aarp.org/work/social-security/info-05–2012/future-of-social-security-proposals.html.

Zygmunt, Joseph F. 1970. "Prophetic Failure and Chiliastic Identity: The Case of Jehovah's Witnesses." *American Journal of Sociology* 75: 926–48.

Index

Abortion, 106–110, 113

Adams, James Truslow, 37–38

Alcohol, 10, 13–15, 17–18, 25n

American Dream, xiv–xv, xxii, 34–66; as myth, 46; mentions of in books, 38–39, 44–45; mentions of by politicians, 38–41; public attitudes toward, 40–41, 52, 62

American Nightmares, xv–xx, 187–191, 193–194

Automobiles, 3–6, 9, 10, 15–17, 21

Bak'tun, 74–76

Behavioral economics, 175–176

Bicycles, 10

CALM (Citizens Against Legalizing Marijuana), 23–24, 26

Career, deviant, 13–15

Cars. *See* Automobiles

Case studies, 31, 193

Children, 25–27, 29–30

Cigarettes. *See* Smoking

Civil War, in collective memory, 141–148, 153–156

Claims: defending popular hazards, 19–22; opposing popular hazards, 22–28

Climate change, 89–96, 98

Collective amnesia, 152–153

Collective memories, 141–144, 147–158

College campuses, 144–147, 150–152, 158

Confederate battle flag, 131–139, 155–157

Confederate symbols, 139–141, 143–146, 155, 157

Crack babies, 121–122

Credit cards, 10, 17

Crimes without victims, 6, 7n

Drunkards Progress (print), 13–15

Economicization, 162–194

Economics, 164–178, 184–186; behavioral, 175–176

Education, and social mobility, 52–54

Equality, 46, 52–57, 64–66, 179–182

Evidence, 70, 90, 96–98, 102

Evolutionary psychology, 172–174, 176

Experts, 159–161, 186

Fallacies, logical, 112–114, 148

Family structure, and social mobility, 54–56

Fatalities: and firearms, 15–16, 23–24; and marijuana, 23, 28; and swimming pools, 26; and terrorism, 24; and traffic, 3–5, 15–16, 24, 25–26

Firearms, 10, 11, 18–21, 23–27, 29–30, 110–114

Foot in the door. *See* Slippery-slope arguments

Future, xix–xx; evaluating predictions about, 69–71, 96–98, 191

Future talk, xxiii, 99–125

Gambling, 10, 19

Global warming, 89–96, 98

Guns. *See* Firearms

Harms, 13–18; harm reduction, 33

Hazardousness (of popular hazards), 9, 12–18, 22–30

Health care, 86, 101, 108, 112

Ideological homogeneity, 182–184

Income. *See* Quintiles, income; Social mobility

Individualism, 61–62

Inequality. *See* Equality

Inertia, 21–22

Intergovernmental Panel on Climate Change, 93–94

Intradisciplinary debate, 177–178, 182–184

Isolation, 155

Libertarianism, 21

Marijuana, 10, 18–24, 26–28, 30

Maya calendar, 71–77, 88, 96–97

Medicalization, 161–162, 185

Medicare, 88, 100, 112, 114

Memorials. *See* Monuments

Metaphors, 118; threshold metaphors, 102

Models, disciplinary, 171–176, 179–181

Monuments, 142–144, 149–150, 157

Motorcycles, 11

Mystification, 99–100

Opposition, 91

Past, claims about, 129–131

Pit bulls, 11, 23–24n

Polyamorous rights movement, 104

Popular hazards, xxi–xxii, 3–33; hazardousness of, 9, 12–18, 22–30; popularity of, 6, 9, 12, 18, 30

Pornography, 10

Practical value, 176–177, 181–182

Predictions, 69–71, 96–98, 191

Presentism, 148

Prohibition, 21n

Psychological harm, 150–151

Quintiles, income, 48–51

Race, and social mobility, 56–57

Religious prophecies, 72–74

Rhetoric, xix, 18–30, 32–33, 38–42, 59, 63, 85, 100–125, 149–150, 192

Risk, 5n, 12–13

Same-sex marriage, 102–106
Slippery-slope arguments, 29,
 100–115, 118
Smoking, 10, 21–22
Social mobility, 46–61, 63, 66;
 absolute standards, 47–49, 51,
 58–59; and American Dream, 35;
 comparative studies of, 58–59;
 and education, 52–54; and
 family structure, 54–56;
 historical studies of, 59–61; and
 race, 56–57; relative standards,
 48–49, 51, 58
Social problems, construction of,
 7–8, 69–70, 129–131, 192–193
Social Security, 77–89, 97–98;
 forecasts of collapse, 78–81;
 public opinion about, 79;
 solutions to, 82–88

Sociology, xx–xxi, 31, 34–36,
 42–45, 63–66, 165–171, 178–186,
 193
Statistical evidence, 23–26
Superpredators, 120–121

Textbooks, 34–36, 49
Threshold metaphors, 102
Time-certain warnings, 71–72
Tip of the iceberg, 115–118
Tipping points, 122–124
Trump, Donald, xvii–xviii, 39,
 187–188
Typifying examples, 22–23, 116

"We're beginning to see," 118–122
Winfrey, Oprah, 35, 47

Y2K, 72–73